IMAGES
of America

DOOR PENINSULA
SHIPWRECKS

IMAGES
of America

DOOR PENINSULA
SHIPWRECKS

Jon Paul Van Harpen

ARCADIA
PUBLISHING

Published by Arcadia Publishing
Charleston, South Carolina

Library of Congress Catalog Card Number: 2006920128

For all general information contact Arcadia Publishing at:
Telephone 843-853-2070
Fax 843-853-0044
E-mail sales@arcadiapublishing.com
For customer service and orders:
Toll-Free 1-888-313-2665

Visit us on the Internet at www.arcadiapublishing.com

*I would like to dedicate this book to my late father,
Roy Paul Van Harpen, who instilled the importance of history to me and
the preservation of it; to my mother, Viola Van Harpen, who inspired
me to achieve my goals and work for them; to my son, Nicholas,
and the rest of my family, for putting up with me.*

CONTENTS

ACKNOWLEDGMENTS

Without the following contributions this book would not be possible, my undying thanks: the Door County Maritime Museum (DCMM), John Moga and June Larson; Thunder Bay Sanctuary Research Collection (TBRC), Patrick Labadie, Marlo Broad, and Wayne Lusardi; University of Wisconsin Superior (UWS), Laura Jacobs; the Door County Public Library, Sturgeon Bay; Historical Museum of Bay County, Michigan, Ron Bloomfield; Jackson Harbor Fishing Museum, Washington Island; Kewaunee County Historical Society; KJB Productions, Kim Brungraber; Wisconsin Maritime Museum, Christine Waterbury; and individual contributions from David Loucks, Gary K. Soule, Bernard Bloom, David DeGroot, Charles Peterson, Carolyn Cane, Elaine Green, Jim Baye, Garrett Van Dreel, Bob LaViolette, Harry Zych, Ralph K. Roberts, and Walter Hirthe. My sincere apologies to anyone I have missed.

INTRODUCTION

Door County abounds in maritime history, which started before the first Euro-American ever stepped foot on this beautiful peninsula. The legend has it that Native Americans had frequent skirmishes between local tribes, and in one instance, a plan to invade the mainland by crossing the body of water at night, between Washington Island and the northern tip, turned into a catastrophe. A fast-brewing summer storm sank the invaders' canoes with great loss of life; after that time, the American Indians called the passage the Door of the Dead. Early French explorers heard of the tale and named it Porte Des Morts. English translation called it Death's Door, from hence the county is named. However, the legend cannot be traced in Native American history.

The first shipwreck of Euro-American decent is Réne-Robert Cavelier, Sieur de La Salle's ship the *Griffin*, which left Washington Island in 1679, never to be heard of again. Although modern technology has for the most part stopped commercial ship accidents in the Great Lakes, it was not prevalent during the expansion of the Midwest after the Civil War. Death's Door, with its fast currents and crossing winds, played havoc with the schooners trying to ply the waters between the bay of Green Bay and Lake Michigan. In 1878, a plan was made to cut a canal between Sturgeon Bay and Lake Michigan. This would save time running from the busy Port of Green Bay to Chicago and also preclude the dangers of going through Death's Door. By 1880, this became a reality.

This book is intended to take the reader on a tour of shipwrecks in the Door Peninsula, starting at Sturgeon Bay and heading into Lake Michigan. From there it travels north up the east coast of the peninsula to Washington Island and back into the bay of Green Bay, and ending back in Sturgeon Bay—nicknamed the "Bone Yard of the Great Lakes." Not only historical by nature, the shipwrecks represent the boom of maritime technology that encompassed this period, from the scow schooner *Ocean Wave* that sank in 1869 to the steel steamer *Bartelme* that ran ashore on Cana Island in 1928.

Door County by name and the abundance of shipwrecks between the Civil War period and the early 20th century would make one think of the great loss of life. Fortunately this is not true for the peninsula, and its biggest loss of life was that of 11 people in a single incident on the packet steamer *Erie L. Hackley*. This can probably be accounted for by the fact that most wrecks were shallow, nearshore strandings, and the heroic work of the U.S. Life Saving Service, now an integral part of the modern-day Coast Guard.

This book only covers a small fraction of the shipwrecks of the county. It is interesting to note the relationships of the men and ships and how they intertwined with each other in everyday life, and at the end.

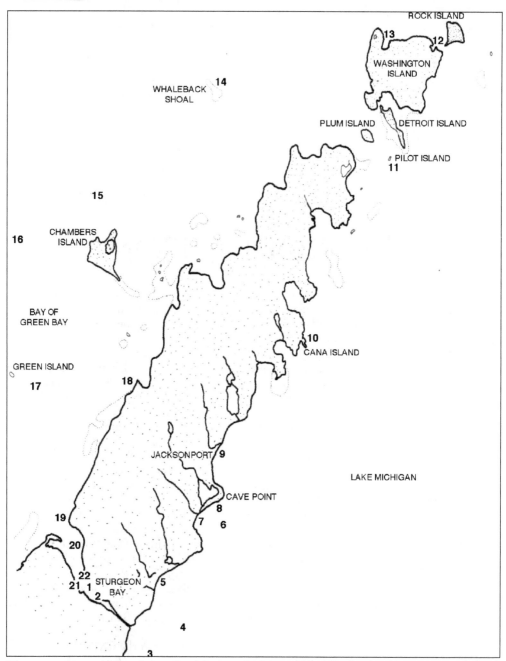

This is a key to the chart: 1. *Adriatic*; 2. *Mary Ellen Cook*; 3. *Ottawa*; 4. *Lakeland*;
5. *City of Glasgow*; 6. *Ocean Wave*; 7. *Otter*; 8. *Australasia*; 9. *Perry Hannah* and *Cecilia*;
10. *Michael J. Bartelme* and *Frank O'Conner*; 11. *Forrest, Gilmore,* and *Nichols*; 12. *Kate Williams*
and *Iris*; 13. *Louisiana, Halsted,* and *Pride*; 14. *R. J. Hackett*; 15. *Alvin Clark*; 16. *May Queen*;
17. *Erie L. Hackley*; 18. *Iver Lawson*; 19. *Joseph L. Hurd, Pewaukee,* and *Vermillion*; 20. *Dan Hayes*;
21. *Oak Leaf, Ida Corning,* and *Empire State*; 22. *Joys, Lucia A. Simpson,* and *Fountain City*.
(Courtesy of Bob LaViolette.)

One

THE JOURNEY BEGINS
STURGEON BAY TO CAVE POINT

Shipwrecks all have their own personal stories to tell. Some involve new technology, others heroic crew or heroic rescues by the lifesavers of the time; yet others tell of a conspiracy to get money from the insurance companies.

This chapter starts out with the schooner *Adriatic*. John Leathem and Thomas Smith, who started Leathem and Smith Towing and Wrecking Company, among other ventures that included a stone quarry and shipbuilding, were its owners. The *Wyandotte* was a steel propeller built in 1908 as a self-unloader, and Smith liked this design. (Although the *Wyandotte* is considered the first self-unloader built exclusively for that purpose, the wooden freighter *Hennepin*, built in 1888, was first to get the self-unloading gear in 1902. The *Wyandotte* equipment was based on this design, so the *Hennepin* was actually the first true self-unloader in the world.) The *Adriatic* was the third self-unloader and the only one built on a schooner hull. Thomas Smith died in 1914, and all companies were renamed Leathem D. Smith Company. Leathem worked at modifying the design on the *Adriatic* and came out with his own patent for self-unloading gear in February 1923, and another in 1928.

It is interesting that one of the crew of the *Ottawa*, seaman Peter Buset, was picked up in Chicago, and it was his first trip on the Great Lakes. His seabag was found by the lifesavers on the beach and in it first-class master's papers for ocean sailing along with $500 cash. He was going to send for his family in Norway as soon as he made enough money. The schooner *Mary Ellen Cook* had wintered with the *Ottawa* in Chicago and had left about the same time. The captains were good friends, and seaman Frank Vanefins of the *Ottawa* had a brother aboard the *Cook* at the time.

For the steamer *Lakeland*, a dive team was assembled out east to explore the wreck in 1925. Along with doing the investigation, the navy was testing a new helium-air mixture that had only been used on guinea pigs in chambers. The mixture consisted of 90 percent helium and 10 percent oxygen and was supposed to help prevent the bends. In the summer of 2005, Dan Woelfel, who has a cottage in Whitefish Bay, Wisconsin, found a wreck in the bay while jet-skiing; within the month, it was identified as the *Australasia*.

The *Adriatic*, a three-masted schooner, was built in 1889 by Capt. James Davidson in West Bay City, Michigan. The schooner was 202 feet in length, a 34.7-foot beam with a 16.6-foot depth, 915.67 gross tons, and an 869.89 net. Thomas H. Smith purchased the vessel for $1,000 in early November 1912, and it was his intention to use the craft for hauling crushed stone from the start. According to the *Advocate* files, November 7, 1912, "She will be brought here this fall where she will undergo an overhauling and remodeling to be put into the stone trade, it being the intention of the new owners to use it for transporting the product from the crushing plant. A traveling derrick will be put on the craft and the stone unloaded with a clam shell, the cargo being carried in the hold, which will be arranged for that purpose." (Courtesy of TBRC.)

The *Adriatic* is seen loading iron ore at Escanaba ore docks. The early part of the 20th century brought new developments in shipping, and the move to self-unloaders was in its infancy. Thomas Smith's son Leathem D. Smith had graduated from the University of Madison with a degree in civil engineering in 1909 and went to work with his father in Sturgeon Bay. The *Adriatic* would be their vehicle for testing and improving some of the first self-unloading innovations on the Great Lakes. (Courtesy of UWS.)

The *Adriatic* had many mast configurations during its life as a schooner. According to the *Advocate* files from December 5, 1912, "It is proposed to build hopper bins in the hold of the vessel for carrying crushed stone, and it is estimated that she will accommodate about 1000 or 1200 yards as she carries 1800 tons of coal. A traveling derrick will be put on deck, tracks running the length of the boat on each side of the hatchways. The stone will be unloaded in ten or twelve hours." (Courtesy of DCMM.)

The *Adriatic* is seen receiving its self-unloading gear at the Leathem and Smith shipyard in Sturgeon Bay. At this time in history, unloading at newly developing ports was a primary concern, for manpower was not always available, and when it was, its cost and time was expensive to boat owners. (Courtesy of DCMM.)

On August 27, 1920, Capt. Albert Braunsdorf, his wife Ella, and their 7-year-old daughter, Mabel, were all asleep on the *Adriatic*. The vessel was lying at the Sixteenth Street gate entrance to Manitowoc Shipbuilding Company, where it was engaged in hauling coal between Manitowoc and Two Rivers. With the circus in town, there was a scare the previous evening when someone tried to kidnap Mabel. The captain ordered all gangways removed between the dock and the boat for security, but the self-unloading boom still hung sideways over the dock. (Courtesy of Elaine Green, Mabel's daughter.)

The *Adriatic* is seen here after being converted into a self-unloading barge. Note the loading boom (in center of the photograph) that landed on Captain Braunsdorf. Although this equipment worked well, when the boom was over the side it created a substantial list to the vessel. At about 4:00 in the morning, a night watchman for the yard noticed fire in the forward part of the ship. With no way to get on board, the watchman threw rocks at the rear cabins to alert the crew. Captain Braunsdorf—half awake—scrambled onto the deck, sat down to put his shoes and glasses on, and when he got up, the loading boom fell and landed on him, only coming to a stop when it hit the rail of the ship or it would have crushed him completely. He was on his way to awaken the crew in the forward cabin and forgot that he had let them go ashore for the evening. When the crew arrived, they found the captain unconscious under the wreckage. Captain Braunsdorf received a fractured skull, internal injuries, and his legs were badly broken. Gangrene set in a few weeks later, and despite one of his legs being amputated to stem its spread, he died on October 2, 1920, at the age of 35. (Courtesy of DCMM.)

Pictured is Capt. Albert Braunsdorf's casket at his wake. Note the anchor wreath honoring his service on the Great Lakes. He had been captain and his wife, Ella, was the cook on the *Adriatic* since 1916. Ella and daughter Mabel left the ship, and eventually Ella married her husband's brother, Joseph, and had two more children (common at the time). (Courtesy of Elaine Green.)

The *Adriatic* is seen as it looked after the fire at Manitowoc. Having suffered about $2,000 in damage, it would be hauled back immediately to Sturgeon Bay and rebuilt. (Courtesy of DCMM.)

The *Adriatic* is seen in this postcard dated August 18, 1924, using its self-unloader to make a beach at the Door County Country Club (now the Leathem Smith Lodge). This is believed to be the only picture in existence of an early self-unloader in use. The schooner *Mary Ellen Cook* can be seen at the left. (Courtesy of David Loucks.)

The *Adriatic* is still sunk off of Bay Shipbuilding in Sturgeon Bay. It served well for Leathem Smith, and its enrollment was finally surrendered at the port of Milwaukee on June 24, 1930. Cause of surrender: "Dismantled and Abandoned." The *Adriatic* was abandoned at the Smith Coal Dock, which is now the south yard at Bay Shipbuilding, and lies today in between the pilings where the floating dry dock is stored in the winter months.

One schooner that has its name embraced in Great Lakes history and lore is the schooner *Mary Ellen Cook*. It was built at Grand Haven, Michigan, by R. W. Loutit in 1875. It was 118 feet in length, 25 feet in beam with a 7-foot depth of hold, at 132.89 gross tons, and had three masts. (Courtesy of TBRC.)

This may be the *Mary Ellen Cook* coming over the breakwater. In May 1883, the *Cook* was bound for Chicago with a full load of lumber when it got caught in a nor'easter and took its "wild ride." Capt. Val Valentine got caught in the trough of the seas, and it was impossible to get the schooner through the small entrance of the breakwater, which was not yet finished leaving a spot for a pier with rocks piled to the water level. Captain Valentine devised a bold plan in which he had the centerboard raised as he steered his vessel right for the gap in the break wall. A wave picked up the bow and brought it over the rocks while a second wave pushed it over unharmed in front of a few hundred amazed spectators. Stories told years later by sailors have it that the vessel's cook panicked and jumped overboard and drowned. (Courtesy of DCMM.)

The *Mary Ellen Cook* is seen loading at Chicago. A different version from the *Chicago Tribune* dated May 22, 1883, although not as fantastic, seems much more palatable. Capt. Ed Williams of the *Cook* was coming from Ludington, Michigan, and a storm kicked up as they reached Chicago at about 10:00 p.m. He mistook the red light of a schooner in front of him for the end of the breakwater. As he drew nearer, a wave picked the vessel up, and it was launched on top of the breakwater briefly until a second wave shoved it over. During the commotion, a friend of the captain's son, Henry Miller, who came onboard for the pleasure of crossing the lakes, panicked and jumped overboard and drowned. Captain Williams registered a complaint about there being no lights at the entrance of the breakwater, which would have prevented the mishap and the boy's death. (Courtesy of TBRC.)

The *Cook* did suffer some damage in the accident, and when it was being towed to the dry dock, the tow line parted, crushing the chest of one of the sailors. This event would put the *Mary Ellen Cook* into the legends of the Great Lakes. (Four other sailors from different vessels lost their lives in that storm.) Although the *Cook* would get stranded a few times, it lived a pretty usual life for a working schooner of its time. (Courtesy of DCMM.)

In 1923, the schooner *Mary Ellen Cook* was retired and used as a pier in front of the Door County Country Club. In late July 1927, a fire broke out in the cabin, and the transom fell into the bay. The stern of the vessel was rebuilt but not to original size, just as a dock for boats. In 1934, the vessel was in such bad shape it could no longer be used as a dock and was set on fire. Today, just past the end of the pier, at the Leathem Smith Lodge, lay the scattered remains of the once proud vessel. (Courtesy of DCMM.)

One of the largest maritime disasters to happen south of the Sturgeon Bay Canal was that of the schooner *Ottawa* (second from left) that stranded on April 13, 1911, and lost its crew. The *Ottawa* was built at Grand Haven, Michigan, in 1874 by R. W. Loutit and was 113 feet in length, 25 feet in beam and 7.5-foot depth of hold, and 163.29 gross tons. It was said to have been the first vessel with wire rigging and to be the finest vessel of its time on the Great Lakes. The *Ottawa* had just been fitted out for the season in Chicago and went to Manistique, Michigan, for a load of lumber. On the return trip, it encountered an early spring southeaster that swept this side of Lake Michigan with gale force and created many blankets of fog. The *Ottawa* fetched up just north of Stoney Creek Reef and off of Capt. Christian Braunsdorf's farm on the Door and Kewaunee county line. The *Advocate* quoted Captain Braunsdorf's account of the disaster, April 20, 1911: "About five o'clock Thursday morning I was awakened by a storm, which forced open a door. Getting up, I went out to the barn to see if everything was all right and on my way glanced out on the lake and saw what I thought to be the outlines of a vessel thru the hazy mist . . . I got a range on the boat with a fence post and she appeared to be moving, though slowly. Suddenly the vessel disappeared, a bank of heavy fog having drifted in and shut her out of view. I rubbed my eyes to see if I was dreaming or awake. I went back to the house and thought no more of the vessel, which I supposed was all right." (Courtesy of DCMM.)

The *Ottawa* sits on shore near Foscoro just south of Clay Banks a few days after the incident. The barge *Dohearty* is seen to the left of the bow. The *Advocate* continued with Captain Braunsdorf's tale: "I went out on the farm to work about 9 o'clock. A little after ten o'clock my daughter came running and said there was lumber coming ashore. I quickly got a horse and putting the girl on his back told her to ride fast to our neighbors, Chan. Mackey, and telephone the life-saving station . . . I ran down to the shore with my sons Christian and Joe and we signaled the men on the vessel by waving our arms so they would know help had been sent for. Then the fog closed in around the boat and we couldn't see her any more. A big sea was rolling and as we only had a small skiff could do nothing. Pretty soon we saw an object coming ashore in the fog and as it got nearer the boys waded in and pulled it ashore. It was the Ottawa's yawl boat. We knew then that the crew were all lost if they tried to get ashore in that boat. My wife and Mrs. Mackey walked down the beach and a little while after they saw the body of one of the crew on the beach and pulled it out of the water. Then a second and a third came ashore. By this time the life-savers came, as well as a number of farmers. The fourth body did not come ashore until 9 o'clock at night and the last one four or five hours later. We tramped the beach all night . . . The wreck was half a mile from shore and the water so cold the men could not swim long in it." (Courtesy of DCMM.)

The tug *Hunsader*, from the Leathem and Smith Towing and Wrecking Company, helped in the salvage efforts of the *Ottawa*. The salvagers had tried to pump the *Ottawa* out, to no avail, and it was stripped of its rigging and the wood cargo lightered to the barge *Dohearty*, and then placed on the schooner *Mary Ellen Cook* for transport to Chicago. The vessel was valued at $2,000 and was owned by the Roper Lumber Company and Captain Weborg. The cargo was valued at $3,000. (Courtesy of DCMM.)

The *Dohearty* is seen here. The lifesavers deduced at the time that the accident had happened about 6:00 or 7:00 that morning, and the crew had prepared for a long stay on the boat but thought the schooner was going to go to pieces and fled the vessel prematurely. Their yawl boat probably capsized, and the men succumbed to the cold. The lifesavers said if the crew would have stayed on the *Ottawa* an hour longer they would have been saved easily. (Courtesy of DCMM.)

The steamer *Cambria* (later renamed *Lakeland*), known as "Door County's Car Wreck," is pictured at the Escanaba iron docks. There is probably no wreck talked more about in Door County than the steamer *Lakeland* and the cars in its hold lying on the bottom. It was built of steel in 1887, at Globe Iron Works in Cleveland, Ohio, as a bulk freighter for the Mutual Transportation Company. One of the finest vessels of its time (steel being relatively new as hull material for the Great Lakes), it was 280 feet in length, 40 feet in beam and had a 20-foot depth, with a gross tonnage of 1,878.10, net 1,377.33.

The *Lakeland* is seen shortly after the conversion to a package freight/passenger propeller at the Soo Locks. It originally looked much like its wooden predecessors with a forward pilothouse, three masts, and a single stack. In 1897, at Cleveland, it would receive a rig change that resulted in the removal of the center mast as to enable easier cargo transferees. In 1910, it was sold to the Port Huron and Duluth Steamship Company out of Port Huron. The new owners added side-loading doors and a second deck for staterooms to accommodate passengers and renamed it the *Lakeland*. (Courtesy of DCMM.)

The *Lakeland* is pictured loading cars at Cleveland, Ohio. The steel hull of the *Lakeland* had been bothered by some leaks during the 1924 sailing season. Early that December, the *Lakeland*, now owned by Tri-State Steamship Company of Cleveland, was bound for Detroit from Chicago when the captain received reports of a southwest storm brewing over Lake Michigan. (The *Lakeland* had been engaged in carrying cars from Detroit to Cleveland, Milwaukee, and Chicago, with a capacity of 250 cars.) The captain put into Sturgeon Bay to avoid the storm and stayed all day Tuesday, December 2. At 7:10 the following morning, they departed for Detroit. About 15 miles east of the canal, a leak was discovered amidships, and the pumps were ordered to be run at full force. But the hold filled with water rapidly and Capt. John McNeely ordered the SOS, which was received by Coast Guard watchman Earl Delorme. The vessel came full about, and the captain ran for shallow water. The boiler could not produce enough steam for the engine and pumps running at the same time, so an order was given to check down the engine. Capt. Robert Anderson of the canal station and fellow guardsmen departed the station in a cutter for the scene. Meanwhile the *Lakeland* developed a bad list to port and Captain McNeely ordered 23 of the 27 crew onboard into the lifeboats while he and three officers did what they could to save the doomed vessel. The car ferry *Ann Arbor 6* heard the SOS, came to assist, and took the seamen aboard. By the time the Coast Guard arrived, the ship was in dire straits, and Captain Anderson ordered Captain McNeely and his three officers off the vessel and into his cutter. (Courtesy of TBRC.)

The *Lakeland* starts to settle in the calm water. It made its death plunge at 11:30 a.m., sinking stern first, breaking amidships and blowing the cabins and hatches almost 40 feet in the air. The *Ann Arbor 6* landed the *Lakeland*'s crew at the Goodrich Dock in Sturgeon Bay while Captain Anderson and the officers from the *Lakeland* searched the freezing waters for floating wreckage for nearly two hours. The ship was lost in 210 feet of water, six miles east of the canal. The *Lakeland* was valued at $500,000 and its cargo of 40 Nash and Kissel cars at $45,000. (Courtesy of Wisconsin Maritime Museum.)

The *Lakeland* starts its descent to 210 feet. What would seem to be an open and shut case was far from it. A number of questions bothered the underwriters. Why did the freighter sink in such calm weather? The Thompson Transit Corporation was in deep financial problems; did they sink it for the insurance claim? There were no passengers on this trip, and the insurance would run out in less than a week. (Courtesy of Wisconsin Maritime Museum.)

The *Ann Arbor 6* was the first vessel to render assistance to the sinking *Lakeland*. The insurance companies spent little time getting to the investigation of the sinking. S. D. Foster, attorney from a Detroit firm that represented the underwriters of the ill-fated *Lakeland*, was in the city the following week. He interviewed the Coast Guard and local fishermen and came to the conclusion that most of the cars were probably pushed into a tangled mess and that the boilers also exploded, making salvage of the vessel or cargo in 210 feet of water not feasible. A typewriter desk, four lifeboats, and a few minor articles were all that was recovered by the Coast Guard from the floating debris. The rest of the wreckage drifted on the shore at Algoma. By mid-August, a dive team was assembled to search for clues at 210 feet—no small task in 1925. The crew consisted of 22 professionals, including two navy divers. Hampered by bad weather, it took the five-member dive team about three weeks to complete the diving operations. The insurance companies spent little time getting the case to court; only six weeks elapsed from wrapping up the underwater investigation until the trial in Cleveland. The insurance companies had a good argument but could not, however, prove collusion between Capt. John McNeely and the Thompson Transit Corporation—and they lost the case. (Courtesy of DCMM.)

Above, diver Bob LaViolette is measuring the bell on the sunken wreck. Below, a car is seen in the hold of the *Lakeland*. The *Lakeland* was found again in the late 1970s by diver Kent Bellrichard. An attempt to raise one of the cars was made by Bellrichard, Bob Aznoe, and a group of divers. Raising a car from the inside of a ship down 200 feet is by far no easy task. The plan involved attaching a large oil drum to the car and then slowly filling it with air to pump out the water, and the car would than raise to the surface. (Courtesy of Garrett Van Dreel.)

The salvage boat *Challenge*, seen in the background, was used in the raising. Here the wrecker hauls the frame of the Rollins with the oil drum still attached out of the water. All was well until about 100 feet from the surface a line parted and the car tumbled back down to the bottom. Next a line was reattached, but from the fall, the body of the car tore away on the second attempt. They brought the remains to the west-side dock, and Virgil Mueller used an automobile wrecker to pull the battered frame onto shore. (Photograph by Chan Harris.)

The odometer from the Rollins shows 22 miles and 19.2 miles on the trip meter. What remained was a frame, engine, drivetrain, fender, headlight, wheels, and dash. What was interesting was that the car was not a Nash or Kissel, which were reported to have gone down on the *Lakeland*, but a new 1924 Rollins that was made in Cleveland and not listed on the manifest. (Photograph by Chan Harris.)

Bob Aznoe (left) and Kent Bellrichard pose with the brass whistle from the *Lakeland* shortly after its raising over the Fourth of July weekend in 1980. Never since has a car been raised from the freighter, which has been illegal since 1987, and the steamer now is a tourist attraction for the advanced scuba diver willing to take the risk and explore the cold, murky depths of Lake Michigan. So rests the Lakeland and the enduring legacy of the steamer full of cars some six miles off the canal. (Photograph by Chan Harris.)

The *City of Glasgow*, which had two lives, is seen here sometime between 1889 and 1895. The keel for the *City of Glasgow* was laid in late summer of 1890, and the vessel was one of four large steamers being built by pioneer shipbuilder James Davidson at his yard in West Bay City, Michigan. The vessels would get the nickname the "Big Four," being the largest steamers on the lakes at that time. The *Glasgow*, along with its sister ship, the *City of London*, would be 297 feet in length, and the *City of Berlin* along with the *City of Paris* would be 298 feet in length. (Courtesy of Patrick Labadie.)

Capt. Hugh Stevenson and wife dine aboard the *City of Glasgow*. The *Glasgow* would be launched May 16, 1891, supposed to go in at 4:00 p.m. sharp. At 3:50 p.m., the stern ropes broke because of the strain on them, and the remaining ropes where cut in a hurry so as not to get the ship hung up on the launch ways. The stern already broke water when the bow started its decent; it was a very uneven launch but proved a success. (Courtesy of Port Huron Museum.)

The *Glasgow*'s original dimensions where 297 feet in length with a 41-foot beam and 20.5-foot depth of hold, 2,002.86 gross tons, and 1,672.03 net. Its power would come from a new triple expansion engine that produced 1,175 horsepower, powered by two Scotch boilers that developed 150 pounds of pressure. It was rigged with three masts, one stack, and a plain head and round stern. In its early years, it would tow the schooner *Adriatic* as its consort. (Courtesy of Patrick Labadie.)

The *Glasgow* is seen at the Soo Locks. James Davidson sold it to Capt. Charles L. Hutchinson in October 1895. Hutchinson had just organized the Buckeye Transportation Company, and the *Glasgow* would be the first of the fleet. In 1901, it was rebuilt, and the main deck was raised two feet and the first deck eliminated to increase the gross tonnage to 2,400 tons. The *Glasgow* had few problems, but 1907 would be the end of the once proud steamer. (Courtesy of Patrick Labadie.)

The *City of Glasgow* is seen here sometime between 1897 and 1901. On November 28, 1907, the *Glasgow* would get stranded on the Peshtigo Reef, and the following day, the tugs *W. S. Taylor* of Green Bay and *O. M. Field* of Marinette would lighten some coal and release it for its trip to Green Bay. The *Glasgow* unloaded its cargo of 3,500 tons of coal there and, on December 3, would leave to pick up iron ore at Escanaba for its return trip. On the way out, it ran aground, and the *Taylor* once again came to its assistance, releasing it an hour before fire broke while still in the channel. (Courtesy of DCMM.)

The *Glasgow* is seen here between 1901 and 1907. Capt. J. A. Logan said, "The fire started so far as I can remember just before 4 o'clock . . . The north wind was so strong that it forced the smoke and flames back into the engine room and [the engineers] could not remain at their posts, and the pumps could not be worked. Everyone on board kept his head and there was little danger at any time. The boys battled with the flames until we could see that the fire fighting was useless and we lowered a yawl boat and left the Glasgow. Captain Dennis used a fire hose on the Taylor but could not get close enough to the Glasgow without endangering his own boat to do any good." (Courtesy of DCMM.)

The burned-out hull of the *Glasgow* is pictured after being towed to Sturgeon Bay. The *Glasgow* was now blocking the channel to the Port of Green Bay, and in January 1908, the Leathem and Smith Towing and Wrecking Company was awarded a contract for $900 to remove the vessel by the opening of navigation in spring by the War Department. (Courtesy of DCMM.)

Here is the view inside the burned hull of the *Glasgow* looking to the stern. It was a huge undertaking with many difficulties, but they succeeded, and in May 1908, the *Glasgow* would be towed to Sturgeon Bay and docked at the wharf at the end of Liberty Street. In August of that year, the *City of London* would strand on Dunlap Reef just an eighth of a mile from the burned-out hull. (Courtesy of DCMM.)

The *City of London* was sister ship to the *City of Glasgow*. Thomas H. Smith would salvage the *Glasgow*, but it took too long, and he had to pay for a channel to be dug around the burned vessel as to free up the Port of Green Bay for commercial passage. His $100-a-day fine for being late on the removal totaled $2,800 (for a $900 job). (Courtesy of UWS.)

Putting on the new stern section of the *Glasgow* is possibly Thomas H. Smith (with top hat) inspecting the work. Once the vessel was back to Sturgeon Bay, the boilers, engine, and other machinery were salvaged. The engine was rebuilt at the Hunsader Machine shop, which Smith had interest in, and after nearly a year and a half, Smith decided to make a stone barge out of the *Glasgow* hull, putting a new deck and forward and stern cabins on it. (Courtesy of DCMM.)

The tug *John Hunsader* tows the barge *City of Glasgow* and barge *Mike Dohearty*. It was finished in the spring of 1911 and reenrolled at the port of Milwaukee on April 20, 1911, as a barge with one deck, no masts, plain head, and a square stern. Its new dimensions were 196.5 feet in length, 39.9-foot beam, and 15.6 depth of hold at 958 net tons—considerably smaller than the original vessel. (Courtesy of DCMM.)

Thomas Smith had just finished the new tug *John Hunsader* the previous fall and now, foreseeing a bad year in the stone business, decided to lease some of his fleet to Ashtabula Dock and Dredge Company in Cleveland. The tug *John Hunsader*, the barge *City of Glasgow*, and *Mike Dohearty* would leave for Ashtabula in May 1911. (Courtesy of Door County Public Library.)

This aerial view shows the *City of Glasgow* in Lilly Bay. In late September 1917, the *Glasgow*, loaded with stone, would sink at the Leathem and Smith dock. A portion of the cargo was taken off, and it was pumped out, raised, and recaulked. The tug *Hunsader* picked up the *Glasgow* in Milwaukee, and on October 6, 1917, picked up the *Adriatic* in Two Rivers. The three rounded Two Rivers Point when the seas began to freshen, and by the time they reached the canal, the entrance had built to a full gale. The new captain aboard the *Hunsader*, Harry Searfuss, decided to shorten the towline and in the process the line parted, leaving both vessels adrift. The two barges dropped their large anchors, and the *Adriatic* was holding but the *Glasgow* was dragging. The towline between the two tripped the anchor of the *Adriatic*, setting it free once more. It hung up on a reef, but the *Glasgow* drifted almost to the beach before stopping. The Coast Guard crew from the canal station set out for the wrecks immediately and was successful in retrieving the *Glasgow*'s crew, which consisted of Chas. Wilman and Tom Torstenson. The *Adriatic*'s crew of six was not so fortunate. The Coast Guard could not get alongside the stranded vessel, where they were forced to spend the night. A few days later, the *Adriatic* was pulled off and repaired, but the *Glasgow* was so far in, they worked for a year, on and off, with no luck. Leathem D. Smith fired the captain and first mate of the *Hunsader* after the ordeal and finally abandoned the *Glasgow* in 1922. So ended the second and final life of the *City of Glasgow* after 26 years on the Great Lakes.

This photograph shows the bow of the submerged *Ocean Wave*, featuring the anchor and conventional scow schooner construction. Mark Weborg and Jim Laughlin of Ellison Bay were off of Whitefish Bay on the fish tug *Robin B.* in August 2003 when they pulled up their nets to find a 50-foot-plus mast entangled. They immediately cut the mast out and let it go back to the bottom, marking the location. (Courtesy of Kim Brungraber.)

Here is the cabin on the *Ocean Wave* site. In June 2005, Randy Wallander and Mike Mellon from Manitowoc were the first to dive the new wreck, in 106 to 108 feet of water about two miles northeast of Whitefish Point. Wallander had said, "Visibility was fantastic and about 25 to 30 feet down you could see the entire wreck below you." A historical search was needed to give the wreck an identity. (Courtesy of Kim Brungraber.)

This is the scow schooner *Helen* entering the Manitowoc pier heads in 1880. (This had a bow more closely resembling typical schooner construction; with the exception of being a little longer than the *Ocean Wave*, it was much the same.) With no information about the found wreck other than it was a sailing vessel and its location, Russ Lietz of Waupaca and Jon Paul Van Harpen, the author, tried to figure out what vessel it could be. Since it was carrying stone, the quarry fleets from Sturgeon Bay were checked out, but none had sank near this location. A search of the *Advocate* database again came up empty handed. Other quarries located in Door County also shipped stone—mainly Garrett Bay, Toft Point, and Washington Island. Further database searches provided a quandary—two *Ocean Waves* were operating at about the same time in Door County, a 132-foot barque and a 73-foot scow schooner. Both ships sank within 10 days of each other in September 1869. The next step was to determine the size and vessel construction of the wreck, so Bob LaViolette and Garrett Van Dreel dove the wreck and measured the length and beam and did more photography and video. What they measured must be the smaller *Ocean Wave*, originally 73 feet long, 20-foot beam and 7-foot depth at 74 tons, with two masts, and built by Robert Chambers at Harsen's Island, Michigan, in 1860. (Courtesy of Jim Baye.)

Diver Russell Brungraber peers into the upper cabin and stern cargo hatch. Meanwhile Bob LaViolette provided more details and video of the wreck to help with the research. Found in the *Advocate* files, March 4, 1869, is the following: "Sunk. We learn from Mr. Carrington of Bailey's Harbor, that the scow *Ocean Wave*, loaded with stone sunk in Lake Michigan off White Fish Bay and ten miles from shore. The crew arrived safe at the Bay." (Courtesy of Kim Brungraber.)

Diver Bob LaViolette measures the bowsprit of the *Ocean Wave*. The divers came up with a measurement of 65 feet from the bow to the aft end of the cabin (the stern of the vessel is damaged and buried in sand) and 20 feet in beam. These measurements are consistent with the small *Ocean Wave* listed in databases, and photography and video confirmed it is of scow construction. (Courtesy of Garrett Van Dreel.)

Pictured is the first enrollment for the *Ocean Wave* in 1860. Circled is the written "Eagle Figure head." Archeologist Keith Meverden from the Wisconsin Historical Society was diving on the *Ocean Wave* and discovered that it had a small figurehead carved in its stempost. This was later traced back to its original enrollment paper, which would lead to positive identification of the *Ocean Wave*. (Courtesy of National Archives and Records Administration, Washington, D.C.)

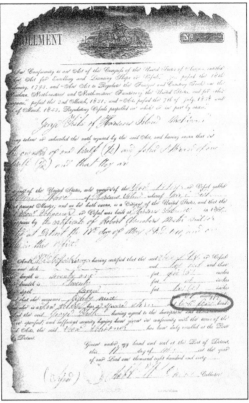

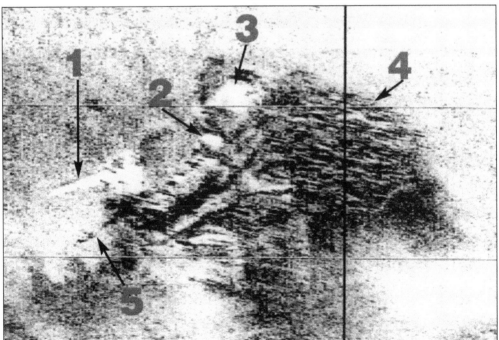

This side scan sonar image of the *Ocean Wave* shows (1) bowsprit shadow, (2) cargo hatch shadow, (3) cabin shadow, (4) stone cargo, and (5) bowsprit. (Courtesy of Harry Zych.)

Visibility on the *Ocean Wave* can exceed 100 feet. The lagging question is, why is the *Ocean Wave* located seven to nine miles closer to shore and almost 260 feet shallower than the good Capt. Fletcher Hackett reported in 1869? Captain Hackett of Milwaukee purchased the *Ocean Wave* on April 16, 1869, and ran the vessel the whole season without insurance. But he did purchase $3,000 worth out of Chicago underwriters three weeks before the loss. It is hard to believe a small nine-year-old scow schooner would be worth $5,000 at the time. Could this miscalculation on distance and depth of water be to mislead the underwriters? Was the sinking just an insurance scam? Or was the captain nervous about hauling stone and bought the insurance? (Courtesy of Kim Brungraber.)

The schooner *Otter* is seen stranded in Whitefish Bay. The United States flag flying upside down in the rigging is a standard call of distress. It was built in 1863 at Newport (Marine City), Michigan. The builder is listed as David Lester. It was listed as being 106 feet in length, 25.83 feet in beam and 11 feet in vessel height, and of 270.68 gross tons with two masts (old measure). On October 9, 1895, after taking on a cargo of wood at the V. Mashek Company pier, the schooner *Otter* was hauled out into the bay and dropped anchor to ride out the approaching storm. It is learned from the *Advocate* files of October 12, 1895 that "She rode out the storm during the night, but about eight o'clock the next morning she broke adrift and as the wind had by this time increased very materially she became helpless as a cockle shell, and soon afterward struck bottom, going ashore nearly opposite the mill. The *Otter* was a vessel of 205 tons gross burden and the property of Ceaser, of Chicago. He also owned the cargo, which consisted of about 130 cords. She was built nearly thirty-three years ago, and become so old and tender that the crew was compelled to spend a good deal of their time at the pumps. It was commanded by Capt. Wm. Kauffmann, and he and his crew were all old sailors who have each seen many years service on both fresh and salt water. They lost everything except the clothes on their backs." (Courtesy of DCMM.)

U.S. Life Saving Service arrives at Whitefish Bay to assist the crew of the stranded schooner *Otter*. Here they are setting up the Lyle gun to shoot a line to the vessel; the lifesavers reached the boat on their first try. "The crew earlier attempted to reach land in the yawl, but this had no sooner been dropped from the davits than it was capsized and torn away from the grasp of the men. The sailors no doubt owe their preservation to this mishap, for had they got into the yawl they would unquestionably all have drowned, as no boat could possibly live in such a storm as was then raging." (Courtesy of DCMM.)

U.S. Life Saving Service hauls Capt. Wm. Kauffmann of the schooner *Otter* in the breeches buoy. "Some of the fishermen made two attempts to reach the crew, but they had been driven back each time. Seeing that it would be impossible to rescue the men with the means at hand, and there was momentary danger of the vessel being battered to pieces, a telephone message was sent to the canal for the life-savers. At the time the men were taken off, the vessel was rapidly going to pieces." (Courtesy of DCMM.)

The U.S. Life Saving Service hauls Captain Kaufman to shore and safety. The following week, salvage operations started on the *Otter*. Its back (keel) was broken so the vessel became a total loss. Its rigging and cargo of wood was salvaged and returned to its owners in Chicago. By December, nothing could be seen of it above water as the elements consumed the doomed vessel. The end of another schooner in the Great Lakes was to the lifesavers, heroes of a bygone era, just another day at the office. The remains of the *Otter*—if ever to be found—probably rest in shallow water not far from the beach near the old mill in Whitefish Bay. (Courtesy of DCMM.)

The *Australasia* loads iron ore at Escanaba, Michigan. The pioneer shipbuilder James Davidson of Bay City, Michigan, built over 100 wooden vessels from 1870 to 1915; of these, at least five lie in Door County waters. The ones located are the *Adriatic, City of Glasgow, Frank O'Connor* (previously the *City of Naples*), and the *E. M. Davidson.* Not located until August 2005 was the *Australasia.* It was the fifth steamer that his yard built and the largest to date. It was 286 feet in length, 39 feet in breadth with a 21.2-foot depth, 1,829.32 gross tons, and 1,539.20 net. It had three masts, two stacks, a plain head, and a round stern. The *Australasia,* when built, was an evolution in wooden steamer design and carried all the latest innovations at the time, including heavy iron strapping, one of the largest steam engines on the lakes, a modern oceangoing steam-powered windlass, and heavy deck hosting equipment. The 3,000-net-ton craft was capable of carrying 100,000 bushels of corn or two million feet of lumber. At a cost of around $153,000, it was a behemoth of its time and the pride of the Davidson fleet. In 1884, Captain Davidson remarked after its launch before a large audience, "She went in as beautifully as anything I have ever saw." (Courtesy of UWS.)

The *Australasia*, seen here loading at Duluth, Minnesota, left Cleveland bound for Manitowoc with 2,200 tons of soft coal. After passing the Straits of Mackinaw on October 17, 1896, Capt. Robert Pringle headed for the west shore of Lake Michigan and into the lee of the north by northwest wind. They sighted land about 6:00 that evening just south of Baileys Harbor. The first watch had just finished supper and the second watch was just about to eat when a fire was discovered between decks. Soon everything on the main deck and forward was ablaze. According to one crew member, little or no effort was made to combat the blaze, only one hose being laid, and it was not used until the fire was out of control. The crew spent most of their time packing their turkeys and belongings until 8:00 in the evening when they took to the small boats. Although the captain prohibited any baggage, several of the crew managed to smuggle theirs aboard the lifeboats. A farmer north of Jacksonport saw the ship ablaze and started a fire on the beach to signal the sailors. After arriving on the beach, the crew made it to Jacksonport and the Erskine Tavern. (Courtesy of UWS.)

The *Australasia* site is pictured from the air—notice the bow toward the top and the stern bottom; the entire amid ship is covered with sand. Word had arrived at the Baileys Harbor Lifesaving Station of the disaster, and they telephoned the Leathem and Smith Wrecking Company of Sturgeon Bay, and Capt. James Tuff immediately departed with a crew of men on the tug *Leathem*. They arrived alongside the *Australasia* at 8:30 p.m., and some men climbed aboard to find the crew's set supper table, taking a quick bite before inspecting the damage.

Here are framing and fastening patterns on the stern of the *Australasia*. The fire reached the stern by the time the men left for the tug. The vessel was headed out to the lake, and Captain Tuff, who thought it would sink in deep water, was able to extinguish the bow and get a line on the vessel around midnight, not before part of its burned bulwarks fell on the tug. The line caught fire and broke eight times, and the fire had to be put out each time and a line reestablished before they could continue. Captain Tuff thought he could pull the vessel to Sturgeon Bay, but it was difficult to control, its rudder being left hard to port.

This diagonal cross bracing, a Davidson trademark, helped in identifying the *Australasia* (the light-colored tube is a three-foot scale). By the time they were abreast of Whitefish Bay, the *Australasia* started to settle, and the *Leathem* towed it into the bay in shallow water and rammed its side to sink it and extinguish the fire at about 9:00 Sunday morning. The *Leathem* then proceeded to Jacksonport to pick up the crew of the burned vessel, where they found them three sheets to the wind. Several scraps broke out between the crews on the way to Sturgeon Bay and one on the dock when they arrived; a few of the *Australasia*'s crew took a beating. Leathem and Smith Towing and Wrecking Company was awarded the salvage contract and worked on the wreck for a year. They salvaged the remaining coal, engine, boilers, and other equipment.

Two

THE JOURNEY CONTINUES
JACKSONPORT TO WASHINGTON ISLAND

This chapter deals with another vessel built by James Davidson, the *Frank O'Connor*. It was originally built as the *City of Naples*. The east coast of Door County has the remains of three Davidson steamers; these represent the evolution of Davidson's wooden bulk carriers. They are the *Australasia* (286 feet, built in 1884), the *City of Glasgow* (297 feet, built in 1891), and the *City of Naples* (301 feet, built in 1892). Anther interesting fact about the *O'Connor* is gleaned from the *Door County Advocate*: "Gardner Karker, of this city, who was firing on the *O'Connor*, remained at his old home here and will stay until the steel strike is settled. This is his second shipwreck within fifteen months but this was the only time in which he landed directly in his old hometown upon being rescued. His other experience was infinitely more exiting. That was the wreck of the cargo steamer *Cream City* which went down near Kitchner Island on Lake Huron in July 1918."

The name Death's Door supposedly came from the Native Americans. They passed it down to the first European explorers, the French, who labeled it to Porte Des Morts, with the English translation of Death's Door. But there is no Native American evidence to place this legend to fact. On modern navigation charts, it is still called the original French, Porte Des Morts Passage; Door County was named after this infamous passage.

Of the three vessels in the picture on page 67 (above), the scow schooner *Forest* was the first to arrive at Pilot Island on the night of October 28, 1891. Capt. George Peters was taking it to Big Bay de Noc, in ballast to retrieve a load of lumber for Chicago parties. It was running before a south-southwest wind. At 9:40 p.m., in the sight of lighthouse keeper Martin Knudsen, it stranded on the southwest reef of Pilot Island. The following morning, the keeper brought in the crew of five, who stayed at the lighthouse for a week while they salvaged the rig of the ship and any other valuables before leaving the island on November 5. That winter, the wreck was pushed onto the rocks of the island, and it became a total loss; its cabin parted, and the ice carried the vessel ashore. The keeper's children would lay claim to this treasure, which they used as a playhouse for years to come.

In this fall photograph of Jacksonport, to the left one can see what is left of the lumber on the banking grounds. Jacksonport is reached by continuing up the eastern coast of the peninsula. In early 1867, a small land company was formed to start logging operations in the area. The three men who formed the company were Andrew Jackson, Col. Charles L. Harris, and John Reynolds. Although Harris and Reynolds actually put up the initial investment, about $14,000, the town of Jacksonport was named after Andrew Jackson, who was the father of the plan to acquire the land for logging business. When they arrived in the area in 1867, they met Perry Hibbard, who owned the property that was needed to build a pier from which to ship their wood products. The land was purchased from Hibbard. Seeing a potential business opportunity, Hibbard built his own pier in 1868, one year before the Reynolds Pier was completed. (Courtesy of Mrs. Stanley Hein; photograph by Fred Erskine.)

Pictured are banking grounds, where lumber men could stack their wood and get credit from local merchants until the schooners would come in spring and purchase the lumber for delivery to Chicago and other ports, now the Lakeside Town Park, sometime between 1910 and 1920. (Courtesy of Mrs. Stanley Hein; photograph by Fred Erskine.)

This plat map of Jacksonport shows, south to north, Reynold's Pier, LeMere Pier, and Hibbard Pier in 1899. The *Perry Hannah*, built in 1859 at Newport, Michigan, by Thomas G. Arnold, was lost in the "Great Alpena Gale" on October 16, 1880, and sunk off Reynold's Pier. It was two-masted, originally 98 feet 8 inches long, with a cargo hold depth of 6 feet 7 inches, and of 210 tons. It was rebuilt in Chicago in 1862 and lengthened to 125 feet by 26 feet by 10.5 feet. (Courtesy of Randall and Williams.)

Seen here are frames from one of the two sunken schooners. It is learned from the *Advocate*, October 21, 1880, that "At Jacksonport the Perry Hannah was driven ashore and is lodged right in the center of the approach of Reynolds' pier, demolishing that structure badly. She will probably be abandoned by her owner, John Long of Chicago . . . The vessel lies in about eight feet of water. Her hold is nearly full of hemlock ties, and there was sufficient stuff on the pier to finish the load, but this has as matter of course, all been washed into the lake." (Courtesy of David DeGroot.)

Pictured are stanchions and rail cap from one of the schooners. "Two cribs in the bridge part of Hibbard's pier were also carried away, but otherwise no damage resulted to that structure. A large amount of stuff, which was on Reynold's pier, lies scattered along the beach and is being picked up as fast as possible." At the time of loss, the *Perry Hannah* was captained by J. Beggs. The enrollment was surrendered at Chicago April 23, 1881. Cause of surrender was total loss. (Courtesy of David DeGroot.)

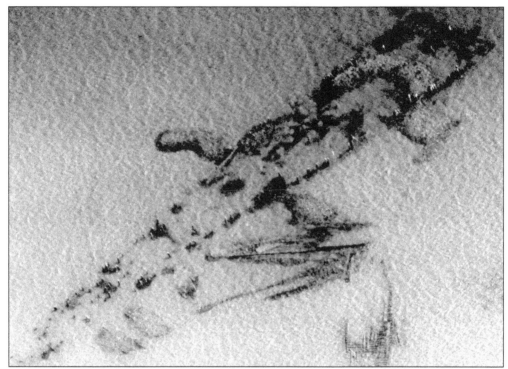

Here is an aerial picture of the Reynolds Pier and the schooners *Perry Hannah* and *Cecilia*. The *Cecilia* was originally built as a barque in 1868 at White Lake, Michigan, by Gregory. It had three masts and was 118.2 feet in length, 25.7 feet in width, and had a cargo hold depth of 8.4 feet, and of 175.82 gross tons. The first owner was J. Larsen, who was also captain. The rig was changed in 1879 to a schooner. It wrecked in a storm on September 8, 1885. The last owner was John Long of Chicago, and it was captained by B. R. Smith, who also had shares in the ship. The enrollment papers were surrendered in Chicago November 13, 1885. Cause of surrender was the vessel was wrecked. The *Cecilia* was worth $4,000.

The Wisconsin Historical Society put a Maritime Trails marker up at Lakeside Town Park in Jacksonport in 2005, after the survey they did in 2004, and the capstan (right) was recovered from an unidentified schooner north of the park.

The *Michael J. Bartelme* was the first steel steamer to be lost in Door County. Built as the *John J. McWilliams* in 1895, it was a state-of-the-art vessel in the new era of steel ship construction on the Great Lakes. Renowned shipbuilder Frank W. Wheeler, at his newly refitted shipyard, F. W. W. and Company in West Bay City, Michigan, thought he had an edge on his bitter rival Capt. James Davidson of Bay City (who built his wooden behemoths until 1903). Wheeler constructed the *Bartelme* to 352 feet in length, 44.66-foot beam, and 22.66-foot depth. It carried 3,400 gross tons, 2,808 net. (Courtesy of TBRC.)

The *Michael J. Bartelme* is seen ashore at Cana Island. Originally sailed by Mitchel and Company in Cleveland, it passed through several owners, was renamed the *M. J. Bartelme* in 1928, and ended with the Valley Camp Coal Company. Valley Camp was not so lucky with the vessel, and shortly after taking it over, its career was ended at Cana Island. (Courtesy of DCMM.)

The *Michael J. Bartelme* is seen after the back was broken and it was partially salvaged. The *Advocate* files, October 5, 1928, report the following: "Ship Ashore Cana Island-The freighter M. J. Bartelme, a 350-footer, went aground about 300 feet off the southeast point of Cana Island yesterday afternoon in a heavy fog and up to this morning had not been released. The tug Leathem D. Smith from Sturgeon Bay was called to give assistance but was unable to reach the wreck until this morning because of a gale from the south. Through its own efforts, the freighter worked from a head on position to broadside by the middle of the afternoon but could get no farther. It is not known how much damage, if any of a serious nature, is done to the hull. The Baileys Harbor coast guards went to the scene when notified from here and stood by." (Courtesy of DCMM.)

The *Michael J. Bartelme* salvage continues. Here the pilothouse and stern upper works have been removed. The *Bartelme* had a crew of 26 and was valued at $300,000 and had been running coal from Ashtabula, Ohio, to Milwaukee and returning from Escanaba with iron ore. The wrecking tug *Favorite* had been sent for from St. Ignace, and Captain Reid of the Reid Wrecking Company of Port Huron arrived. The weather was rough, and before it could be released, the sharp rocks of the island had penetrated the hull plates. By November, the back was broken, and it was abandoned by the underwriters. It was cut up for scrap metal, and by 1938, nothing could be seen of it. (Courtesy of DCMM.)

The *City of Venice*, seen here being launched in 1892, was a sister ship to the *City of Naples* (later renamed the *Frank* O'Conner) and the *City of Genoa*. Fire aboard these early wooden steam bulk carriers was always a threat, and owning to the cargos carried back and forth by these vessels (a volatile mixture of coal and grain), it is not surprising that all three of the James Davidson–built steamers lie in the waters of Door County burned. (Courtesy of Historical Museum of Bay County, Michigan.)

When pioneer shipbuilder Capt. James Davidson died in 1929, little did he know that a ship he had built in 1892 would still be giving enjoyment to people and researchers in the 21st century. The *Australasia* (October 1896), *City of Glasgow* (December 1907), and the *Frank O'Connor* (October 1919) all were carrying coal on their final voyages and all met a similar fate. (Courtesy of Ralph K. Roberts Collection.)

The *City of Naples* (left) is seen with a whaleback steamer in the Manitowoc harbor in 1899. The "Big Four," as they were called in 1891, consisted of the *City of Berlin*, the *City of Glasgow*, the *City of London*, and the *City of Paris*. These wooden steamers were the largest of their time, at 298 feet long. In 1892, the behemoths were succeeded by the second set of ships of the so-called city class that broke the 300-foot mark. These new ships, named after cities in Italy (Genoa, Naples, and Venice), were 301 feet in length.

The *City of Naples* (left) is seen in winter quarters at the Soo, in Michigan. It was sold to James L. O'Connor in 1916 when he started the O'Connor Transportation Company in the midst of World War I. Cargo transportation was at a premium. He named the vessel after his son, Frank, who had worked with him in his ships chandlery business. Frank went on to fight in World War I and was killed in action on May 3, 1918, on German soil. (Courtesy of DCMM.)

The *Frank O'Connor* is seen at dry dock in Buffalo, New York. His namesake was bound for Milwaukee with coal from Buffalo on October 2, 1919, when fire broke out. The *Door County Advocate* reported, "Fire aboard the O'Connor was first discovered about 4 o'clock in the afternoon. It broke out forward and its origin is a mystery. It started either in the forecastle or the chain locker. The oil room and paint locker were both forward but both were in steel compartments. The supposition is that the fire started from a cigarette butt or a match." (Courtesy of TBRC.)

The *Frank O'Connor* is pictured here sometime between 1916 and 1919. The boat was 10 miles off Cana Island when the fire was discovered. The blaze spread rapidly, and the ship was a roaring furnace within a few minutes. It had been carrying grain all season until this trip when it had 3,000 tons of hard coal aboard, and the hold was caked with the dry dust of grain, which burned like tinder. The doomed *O'Connor* was headed for land, and the crew stayed aboard for an hour before the steam steering gear burned, and all control of the boat was lost. (Courtesy of DCMM.)

A diver descends on the triple expansion engine of the *Frank O'Connor*, boiler and condenser at right; the engine rises 25 feet from the bottom. Just as the crew was about to take to the lifeboats, keeper Oscar H. Knudson of the Cana Island Light and his assistant, Louis Picon, gave valuable assistance to the crew, loading the greater part of the baggage in their powerboat and taking the two lifeboats of the *O'Connor* in tow. It was valued at $25,000 and the cargo at $30,000. The O'Connor Transportation Company was sold by the family after the loss. The vessel was located in the 1930s and the cargo of hard coal salvaged by use of a claim shell. (Courtesy of Kim Brungraber.)

Pictured are the rudder, steering quadrant, and propeller, wrapped around which is the steering chain—the cause of the loss of control of the *Frank O'Connor* and abandonment of ship by the crew. Rediscovered in 1990 by mistake by a group looking for the lost schooner *King*, it is now the premier dive site in Door County. (Courtesy of Kim Brungraber.)

Réne-Robert Cavelier, Sieur de La Salle, bids farewell to his ship the *Griffin*, with Fr. Louis Hennepin to his left, on September 18, 1679, never to be heard of again. The legendary Death's Door was notorious for shipwrecks—or was it? It has been proven that the French did over exaggerate the hardships of the Great Lakes, and the possibility exists that this was merely a French concoction to persuade their bitter counterparts, the English, from pursuing endeavors in the western Great Lakes region. (Courtesy of Carolyn Cane; artist Charles Peterson.)

Here is a modern navigation chart of the Porte Des Morts Passage. In the 19th century, hundreds of shipwrecks were reported, but primarily these consisted of groundings, some prolonged, that seldom involved loss of life. Between 1841 and 1899, 17 ships have been unaccounted for—13 schooners, two brigs, one bark, and a scow schooner. There have been many side-scan and proton-magnetometer surveys of this area, and fewer than half the list have been found, and less than half of that positively identified. (Courtesy of National Oceanic and Atmospheric Administration.)

The *J. E. Gilmore* is seen with Plum Island in the background. At this point, the wreckers have already salvaged the main mast. The schooner *J. E. Gilmore*, under the command of Capt. D. B. Smith, came from Chicago empty for Elk Rapids, Michigan, on October 17, 1892. It was entering Death's Door in a bad gale, running with a minimum amount of canvas. When abreast of Pilot Island, the wind shifted to the southwest and threw the *Gilmore* off course and straight for the southwest reef at 11:00 p.m. The waves pushed the *Gilmore* up on a rock shelf very near the wrecked scow schooner *Forest*, which got stranded one year earlier, and broke the back of the once fine schooner. The *Forest*, under Capt. George Peters, had gotten stranded in the sight of lighthouse keeper Martin Knudsen on the southwest reef of Pilot Island. It was the evening of October 28, 1891. (Courtesy of DCMM.)

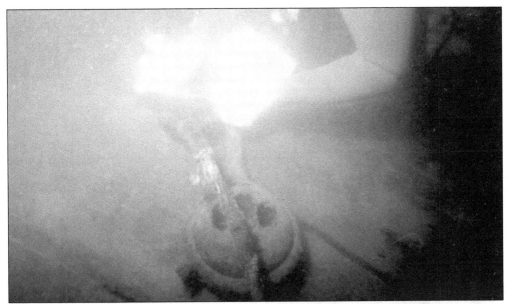

Jon Paul Van Harpen, the author, measures the diameter of a deadeye on the *J. E. Gilmore* site. Note the wire rigging common on post–Civil War schooners. Keeper Martin Knudsen was in contact with the crew and set up the breech buoy just in case, but the cabin of the schooner was dry and safe, and the crew spent the night. They came off the boat the following day and were supposed to go to the mainland by motorboat, but the storm would not subside for 11 days. (Courtesy of David DeGroot.)

Here is an artist's conception of the *A. P. Nichols* under sail. On October 28, 1892, the winds started to gain to a gale force once again. Lighthouse keeper Martin Knudsen and his assistant, Hans Hansen, were on the lookout for ships in trouble. With wind blowing from the west and shifting to the northwest, the schooner *George L. Wren's* and the schooner *Harrison's* anchors were dragging, and before drifting too close to the island, they cut the lines and sailed into the lake. (Courtesy of DCMM.)

The schooners *J. E. Gilmore* (left) and *A. P. Nichols* are seen here, a few years after the salvage crews stripped the vessels of masts and rigging. The schooner *A. P. Nichols* was the next vessel to be spotted by the lighthouse keeper at 2:00 p.m. It was coming from Chicago in ballast to Masonville, Michigan, and attempted to sail through the Door. While tacking in the passage, it missed its stays and dropped the anchor to prevent grounding on Plum Island. The wind was now at full gale force, and it slipped or lost anchor, its foreboom and main gaff broke in the force of the wind and the mizzen topsail and raffee sail carried away. It managed to get to the lee of Plum Island and drop the 1,400-pound anchor. Even with all 600 feet of chain paid out, it started to drag toward Pilot Island. At about 8:00 that evening, a loud crash was heard by the keepers in the lighthouse that announced the arrival of the *Nichols* to the island. They would hold a ladder on the forward deck of the *Forest* until the *Nichols* would do a starboard roll and then hold it while one crew member would get down to safety. There were many harrowing moments, and when Captain Clow Jr., who was the first to jump, fell between the *Forest* and *Nichols*, he was pulled up by his hair by Martin Knudsen and was saved. The next day, the crew took bedding, provisions, and whatever they could salvage, and now the lighthouse had 16 people living in it; about a week later, the seas subsided enough to get the stranded sailors to the mainland. (Courtesy of Walter Hirthe.)

The A.P. *Nichols* (right) was rocking from port to starboard on the stone shelf, and when it took a starboard roll, it almost touched the bow of the *Forest* (center, with men). The *Nichols* came to rest at the bow of the *Forest*, which was sunk with the decks just out of the water. The J. E. *Gilmore* is seen on the left. (Courtesy of Walhter Hirthe.)

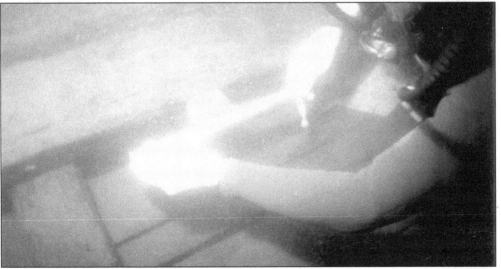

Jon Paul Van Harpen, the author, measures a wood cleat on the site of the J. E. *Gilmore*, which rest in 60 feet of water farther out from Pilot Island. The *Forest* was built at Newport, Michigan, by and for David Lester in 1857. It was 87.5 feet long, with a 22.25-foot beam, and had two masts. It was rebuilt to 115.6 feet long and a 23-foot beam, with three masts. The J. E. *Gilmore* was built in 1867 at Three Mile Bay, New York, by Asa Wilcox. It was 137.7 feet in length, with a 25.4-foot beam, and had two masts. The A. P. *Nichols* was built as a barque in 1861 at Madison, Ohio, by the Bailey brothers. It was 145 feet long, with a 30-foot beam, and had three masts. (Courtesy of David DeGroot.)

Here is an artist's rendering of the tug *Kate Williams*. It was built in 1862 at Cleveland, Ohio, by Ira Lafrinnier. The wood hull was originally 110.5 feet in length, with a 20.75-foot beam, and 9.66-foot vessel height at 212.84 gross tons. In the fall of 1901, the *Williams* had a complete rebuild at a cost of $9,000 in Milwaukee, where it would be as good as new. In June 1906, it was sold to Martin Dredging and Dock Company of Menominee, but the inspectors condemned the boiler, so a new one was made. By the fall of 1907, trouble already started to brew for the company, and it would just be the beginning of the end of the *Williams*. While in the harbor, the tug dragged anchors and went on the rocky shore. (Courtesy of TBRC.)

Tug *Kate Williams* is seen on the beach at Jackson Harbor. The *Advocate* reported, "The Leathem & Smith T. & W. Co. have been awarded the contract to raise the *Kate Williams*, which some time ago driven on a reef in Jackson Harbor during a high NW gale. The tug being in charge of the U.S. marshal at the time of the accident the government will stand the expense of releasing her . . . The tug is said to have been pretty badly shaken up during the northwest blows, which have prevailed recently. The craft was carried still further up on the rocky ledge until there is now but 7 feet at the stern, and the tug draws 12 feet. She lays on the side, being in such a position that a person cannot walk on her decks. It is said that the boiler of the steamer has shifted. It is believed by those who have seen the boat that it will be a difficult matter to release her." (Courtesy of David Loucks.)

The *Williams* wreck was a curiosity to the people of Jackson Harbor. Here one can see sightseers rowing out to it. The following week, reports came that the *Williams*'s boiler had not shifted, and the *Williams* was still in salvageable condition. (Courtesy of DCMM.)

Pictured here is the operation of removing the boiler on the wreck of the *Kate Williams*. Weather still hampered the salvage, and the following week, wrecking operations concluded for the year. By the end of March 1908, the Leathem and Smith Towing and Wrecking Company had taken another salvage job from the government, the salvage of the burned steamer *City of Glasgow* that was blocking the entrance to the Port of Green Bay. (Courtesy of DCMM.)

The boiler is being raised and is about to be placed on the scow. By the end of April 1908, the courts ordered a lien on the *Williams* for the wages of the captain, but the *Williams* had not been recovered and was in bad shape with little hope it could be saved. In May, with the wrecking company very busy with the wreck of the *Glasgow* and not ever being paid for the work on the *Williams*, it could not expedite labor, boats, or equipment to complete the salvage. By the end of May, the work on the *Glasgow* was just about finished, but the *Williams* had suffered much damage from the elements. The legal problems were just starting, and the *Williams* was sold by the U.S. marshal in Milwaukee to Thomas Smith for $1,200—the exact amount of money owed to him for his work the previous fall. (Courtesy of DCMM.)

Men work aboard the tug *Smith*, with the wreck and derrick from scow seen in the background. There was still another $400 owed to Leathem and Smith Towing and Wrecking Company, and Captain Hayes was still not paid from his suit. Capt. Hank Tufts, whose work on the *Glasgow* salvage was heralded everywhere, now took on the salvage of the *Williams* amidst mounting legal claims against the vessel. (Courtesy of DCMM.)

The tug *Smith* works on the wreck of the *Kate Williams*. Note the boiler to the left. The *Smith* and a scow that was leased from parties in Menominee would leave again the following week for Jackson Harbor to recover the engine and boiler from the *Williams*. William Binks was now the wrecking master because Captain Tufts took a different position with the Leathem and Smith Company. (Courtesy of DCMM.)

This is diver Pearl Purdy working on the site of the *Kate Williams*. The following week, an accident would delay operations in a dangerous endeavor. According to the *Advocate* files, September 17, 1908, "Diver Pearl Purdy . . . was employed on the *Kate Williams* at Jackson Harbor, being engaged in dynamiting the wheel off the shaft. While standing around on deck Saturday he was inspecting a dynamite cup, carelessly picking at it with a knife. An explosion followed and his finger and thumb were badly torn." (Courtesy of DCMM.)

The *Williams* is viewed on its starboard side, showing where it was patched with the wrecking boom in background. Wrecking operations were completed by the third week in September 1908, and all of the machinery was salvaged with the exception of the boiler condenser, which was broken during the removal of the boiler. The engine and boiler were taken to the Hunsader Machine shop in Sturgeon Bay to be rebuilt. Thomas Smith had invested in this shop, and John Hunsader would get a lot of work from him. In 1910, Smith would start on building a new tug for his fleet, and the rebuilt engine and boiler from the *Williams* would be used in the new tug that was christened the *John Hunsader*. (Courtesy of DCMM.)

The small schooner *Iris* sailed out of Jackson Harbor, Washington Island, for much of the second half of its career. It was built in Port Huron, Michigan, in 1866 and was 74 feet in length, with a beam of 19.2 and a depth of 6.6 feet at 62.18 gross tons. (Courtesy of DCMM.)

The sails on the schooner *Iris* have been repaired a few times. In 1910, the *Iris* was sold to Capt. T. Thompson of Manitowoc for $150. In 1913, the *Iris* was reported by the Merchant Vessel List as being stranded in Jackson Harbor and a total wreck having three on board that reached land safely. (Courtesy of Kewaunee Historical Society.)

The *Iris* wrecked in Jackson Harbor. A local commercial fisherman named Jacob Ellefson, whose family has owned the adjacent property since 1907, told an interesting story of how the *Iris* came to be at Jackson Harbor. The owner of the *Iris* was trying to sell the ship, as it was very old and no longer the most seaworthy of vessels. A local gentleman told the captain he would buy it for $10; however, he was unable to find the money to purchase the *Iris*. The captain, unable to find a buyer with money, brought the *Iris* into the mouth of Jackson Harbor, set all sail, and then sailed as fast as he could, running hard aground next to Ellefson's pier and abandoning the ship possibly for insurance money. (Courtesy of Wisconsin Maritime Museum.)

The small schooner *J. H. Stevens* (left) and the schooner *Minerva* ride out the Big Blow of 1913 in Washington Harbor, while the masts of the schooner *Challenge* can be seen in the background at the Westside Dock. The storm started to give its warnings on Friday, November 7, 1913, but by Saturday, it had turned into a gale of hurricane proportions for the upper Great Lakes region. (Courtesy of David Loucks.)

The storm, which was blowing out of the southwest, persuaded many vessels in northern Door County to seek the refuge of the lee in Washington Harbor, situated on the northwest side of the island. But the *Louisiana* dragged anchor and wound up on the eastern shore of the harbor. Shortly after, a fire was discovered, and after a failed attempt to put it out, the ship was abandoned. The crew was only a short distance from shore and required little assistance from the lifesavers. The *Louisiana* is pictured here as it looked prior to going on the beach at Washington Harbor. (Courtesy of DCMM.)

The *Louisiana* is seen after the fire, its smokestack rising above the wreckage. It was valued at $15,000 at the time of loss. (Courtesy of Jackson Harbor Fishing Museum.)

The burned and salvaged remains of the *Louisiana* sit in Washington Harbor. The Leathem and Smith Towing and Wrecking Company purchased the machinery from the underwriters in 1918, and in 1920, the boiler was finally recovered and the job completed. The *Louisiana* was built at Marine City, Michigan, in 1887 by Morley and Hill. It was 267 feet in length, 39.6 feet in beam, with a 20-foot depth of hold, and of 1,929 gross tons. (Courtesy of David Loucks.)

The steam barge *James H. Prentice* would take its consort, the *Halsted*, into the harbor and allow the vessel to ride its anchors, while the *Prentice* decided to ride the storm out in the lake. The wind switched directions to the northwest, which locked in the vessels that sought its refuge now unprotected from the gale. The *Halsted* started to drag anchor, and the Lifesaving Service on Plum Island was summoned for help. (Courtesy of TBRC.)

The *Halsted* is stranded up on the beach in Washington Harbor. The vessel would lift in the heavy sea, and its anchor would slip but take hold again for about an hour before it lost hold again. This went on for about 20 hours until it was about 60 feet from shore. About 5:00 a.m. on Sunday, the lifesavers, under the direction of Capt. William Robinson, shot a line over to the *Halsted*. Before the breeches buoy could be rigged, a giant wave picked the *Halsted* up and deposited the ship on the beach. (Courtesy of DCMM.)

The *Halsted* is high and dry in Washington Harbor. The crew—shaken—looked about, and although their craft was uninjured, they simply put a ladder to the side and climbed down to the safety of the beach. The lifesavers now had the small schooner *J. H. Stevens* and the larger schooner *Minerva* still at anchor riding out the storm. The lifesavers set up a watch for the two schooners about 3:00 p.m. that Sunday. The winds started to decrease, and the lifesavers, who had been on duty for more than three days, started to pack for home. (Courtesy of David Loucks)

The *Halsted* rests on the beach over the winter of 1913–1914. It was built at Little Sturgeon Bay, Wisconsin, in 1872 by Thomas Spear and launched May 1, 1873. It was 171 feet in length, 33.33 feet in beam, with a 12.33-foot depth of hold, and 496.53 gross tons. Seventeen other vessels in the Great Lakes were totally destroyed during the storm, taking the lives of more than 250 sailors at a price of $5 million in property losses. (Courtesy of DCMM.)

The schooner *Pride* is iced up and on the rocks at Washington Harbor. It was built in Sandusky, Ohio, in 1849. The *Pride* was 87 feet long, with a beam of 26 feet, depth of 6 feet, and was of 83 tons burden. According to the *Advocate* on November 30, 1901, "The schooner *Pride* is a total wreck, now lying on the beach in Washington Harbor, near Matthew Foss dock. In trying to beat out of the harbor at an early hour Friday morning, and being pretty close to shore, the vessel missed stays and before anything could be done to prevent it, she was riding on the rocks. There was some 900 bushels of potatoes and a few cords of wood on the craft, Captain Klingenberg intending to fill out the load with wood at Nor. Shellwicks dock on the east side of the harbor. About 100 bushels of the potatoes were saved from the wreck Saturday by the owners, Lawrence Klingenberg and P.C. Eriksen, who shipped about 400 bushels each and John Johnson 100 bushels. The balance of the potatoes will be a total loss. This is a hard blow to all concerned. The *Pride* is one of the oldest schooners in point of service on the lakes, having been built at Sandusky, O. and came out in 1849. She had a gross measurement of 83 tons and was owned and commanded by Capt. C. Klingenberg of this port." Over time, the *Pride* broke up on the beach and slide into deeper water. Today it rests in 60 feet of water and is an easy dive in Washington Harbor. (Courtesy of David Loucks.)

Three

FROM THE ISLANDS TO THE BAY

WHALEBACK SHOAL TO HORSESHOE BAY

One of the first divers to locate the *R. J. Hackett* was Paul Baudhuin. While diving around Whaleback Shoal, he came across the boiler, located a short distance from the wreck, in 1957. Today, although remote, the *Hackett* provides a great shallow-water dive or snorkel trip, and it is natural breeding grounds for a variety of fish. The *R. J. Hackett*, at 208 feet and built in 1869, was the first generation of wooden bulk carriers in the Great Lakes. The steamer *Louisiana*, at 267 feet and built in 1887, was among the second generation, and the *Frank O'Connor* (formerly the *City of Naples*), at 301 feet and built in 1892, was the third and last generation of wooden bulk carriers. The *Hackett* was to loading ships as the *Adriatic* was to unloading ships.

The schooner *Jenny Bell* was the first old schooner that was attempted to be raised from the bottom of Green Bay. The group only succeeded in getting it to the surface until the vessel slipped from its cables and sank again, destroying the stern and breaking a mast and bowsprit. Although in worse shape, it still remains a good dive today. Frank Hoffman, who had directed that effort, vowed this would not happen to them on the *Alvin Clark* lift. Although the lift was successful, time would not be so merciful on the *Clark*, which by 1979 had been out of the water for 10 years and showing rapid deterioration.

In June 1980, Frank Hoffman found the *Hackley* north of Green Island. He had thought that if he could raise the *Hackley* and put it next to the *Clark*, it would bring in added tourist dollars to help restoration costs. The job had to be done fast and, underfunded, turned out to be another disaster. In the raise, the stern broke, cutting through one of the nylon slings, and the wreck fell back to the bottom; its rudder and a small piece of bulwarks were the only pieces to surface. Charles McCutcheon Jr. measured the entire vessel and created a complete set of building plans for the *Alvin Clark*, which today are the living legacy of the once fine ship. The *Clark* was finally bulldozed and sent to a landfill in 1994. Hopefully, the lesson learned is it is better preserved in the cold freshwaters of the Great Lakes.

The first steam-powered bulk carrier, *R. J. Hackett*, an innovation to Great Lakes bulk carriers, is seen on Lake Michigan. It was designed and built by Elihu M. Peck in Cleveland, Ohio. It featured a forward pilothouse, compact aft cabins with a single center hold, and 24-foot centered hatch openings to match the ore loading chutes at Marquette, Michigan. It was also designed to tow barges or consorts equal or smaller than its own size and carried masts for emergency power or to help ride better in heavy seas. *R. J. Hackett* was launched on November 16, 1869, and was 208.1 feet long, 32.5 feet in beam, 12.6 feet in depth, and of 748.66 gross tons. The *Hackett* proved to be very successful, and the bulk freighters would evolve after its original design. (Courtesy of DCMM.)

On November 12, 1905, the *Hackett* would catch fire on its way to Marinette, Michigan, with a load of coal. Lifesavers from the Plum Island U.S. Life Saving Station went to its assistance. (Courtesy of DCMM.)

Pictured is the steeple compound steam engine of the *Hackett*. According to the *Advocate* files from November 18, 1905, "Steamer Hackett Burns. The steamer R. J. Hackett, Capt. H. C. McCallum, was destroyed by fire on Green Bay Sunday Morning. The steamer was bound from Cleveland to Marinette with a cargo of 1200 tons of soft coal and when in the vicinity of Cedar River fire broke out in the boiler room. Being unable to subdue the flames the boat was run onto Whaleback Shoal and the crew of thirteen men escaped in the lifeboats. The burning steamer was sighted by the crew of the fishing tug Stewart Edward of Detroit, Harbor, Capt. Chas. McDonald, who went to the scene. They picked up the crew and took them to Marinette."

Diver Gary Holbrook examines the shaft of the *Hackett*. Note the large flywheel at upper right. The boat was also seen by the lookout of the Plum Island lifesaving station about 8:15 a.m.; Captain Egle and his crew immediately started for the scene of the disaster, 11 miles distant. Notwithstanding winds dead ahead, they reached the wreck before noon.

The broken propeller on the *Hackett* was a result of a diver in the 1960s attempting to remove it by use of explosives. The after part of the steamer, by the time the lifesaving crew arrived, had burned away. Captain Egle boarded the empty craft and secured the papers of the captain and first officer, and the fire burning beneath subsequently consumed the entire boat.

This steam-powered windlass was recovered by divers in the mid-1960s, and it is now on display at the Gills Rock Maritime Museum. The *Hackett* was valued at $16,000 and the loss on the cargo at about $3,500.

The brigantine *Alvin Clark* is seen after its masts were set and rerigged in the fall of 1969. The *Clark* was built at the Bates and Davis Shipyard in Truago (Trenton), Michigan, in 1846. It was 105.66 feet long, 25.33 feet in beam, with a 9.33-foot depth of hold, and 218.35 gross tons. On June 29, 1864, the vessel came through Death's Door on its way to Oconto, Wisconsin, for a load of lumber. It was light, and the captain wanted the holds cleaned. The cargo hatches were taken off and stored below decks, and the crew took up the chore of sweeping out the hold. They had finished the job when a sudden and fierce storm came up and rolled the vessel over, just north of Chambers Island. Captain Higgie, his first mate, and a sailor working for passage all drowned, and two other seamen where rescued shortly after. (Courtesy of Bernard Bloom.)

The skylight and cabin roof were in remarkably good shape after the *Alvin Clark* was raised. In the fall of 1967, fisherman Dick Grabowski snagged his nets on something near Chambers Island. He contacted diver Frank Hoffman for help, who dove to retrieve the nets and found they were hooked to a remarkably well-preserved wreck. (Courtesy of Bernard Bloom.)

The wheel, when found, still held canvas on it. In the early 1960s, many artifacts from ships were being recovered, but the big prize was to raise one intact, and here was one in pristine condition. The following year, a plan was devised to raise the vessel without destroying it, as had happened in the past; Frank Hoffman vowed this salvage would be a success. (Courtesy of Bernard Bloom.)

Inside the cabin, bunks show what life was like aboard a 19th-century sail craft. The plan was to take the masts out and pump all the silt from the cabin and the hold that had accumulated over a century of submersion. Then holes would be drilled using a suction hose pre-bent to the hull's curvature, cables would be pulled through, and the ship would be raised under a barge. (Courtesy of Bernard Bloom.)

Meanwhile, a local television station took great interest in the project, but Hoffman had no idea what ship they had found, so the news anchor dubbed it the "Mystery Ship." Pictured here are the windlass with assorted blocks and tackle on the bow of the Mystery Ship. (Courtesy of Bernard Bloom.)

Here is the centerboard trunk in the hold of the Mystery Ship, looking aft. It was July 23, 1969, and the barge was in place and the cables were all attached. A hand winch was devised that was geared so that every 100 turns would raise the ship about five inches. Being in 114 feet of water, this was an all-day event. It was brought in under the lift barge to Marinette Marine for the final lift. It was completed, and the crew that made over 3,000 dives without an accident could finally see the whole ship at one time. (Courtesy of Bernard Bloom.)

Here is the forward mast stepped into the keel, just in front of the chain locker. The ship and artifacts were put on public display. A newspaper search found a ship that had sunk in the general location, and a stencil found in the cabin had the initials of the sailor working for passage. The Mystery Ship was identified as the *Alvin Clark*. (Courtesy of Bernard Bloom.)

Artifacts on display at the Mystery Ship Marina told a story of everyday life in the 19th century. Over the years, the ship deteriorated, and debts mounted for Frank Hoffman, who sold the marina with ship in 1985. The new owner leased the marina to Don Gillette, who moved the vessel to the back of the marina with plans to restore it. But hope grew dim, as the marina could not generate the capital it needed to restore the aging craft. (Courtesy of Bernard Bloom.)

The *Alvin Clark* hogged and sagged just a year before its final move. The decks gave way, and it was deemed a public hazard. In 1993, it was bulldozed and brought to a landfill—one of the biggest maritime disasters ever to happen on land.

The collapsed decks of the *Alvin Clark* are seen here. It represented an engineering feat of large proportions in its raising, but at the same time, no long-term preservation plan had been considered. There was a lot of study done and a lot learned about early sail construction. Charles McCutcheon Jr. measured the entire vessel and created a complete set of building plans for the *Alvin Clark*, which was better off preserved in the cold waters of the Great Lakes.

The *Lettie May* was built at Fort Howard, Wisconsin, a year before the *May Queen* and very similar in size and design. Intercoastal trading was the earliest form of getting produce and merchandise between ports in Door and surrounding counties in the post–Civil War period in the Great Lakes. This was accomplished by these small shallow draft schooners that could navigate the undeveloped rural harbors, before the age of packet/passenger freighters. (Courtesy of Walter Hirthe.)

Here is one of the intact fish barrels on the *May Queen*, which carried the cargo bound for Menominee. It was built in 1875 by master carpenter Ivy Philbrook in Menekaunee (now Marinette), Wisconsin, for E. B. Graham of Fish Creek. It was listed as 38.3 feet in length, 12.2 feet in breadth, 4.6 feet in depth, 12.12 tons capacity under tonnage deck, and 0.91 tons capacity above tonnage deck for a total of 13.03 gross tonnage. It had one deck, two masts, a plain head, and a square stern. (Courtesy of Kim Brungraber.)

An anchor from the *May Queen* is buried in the bottom of Green Bay, covered by zebra mussels. The loss of the *May Queen* was reported in the *Advocate* on December 14, 1882: "Loss of the May Queen. The little schooner May Queen, owned by John Lindquist, of Menominee, [John Lindquist was never on any paperwork as owner] foundered a week ago Monday about twelve miles north of Menominee, and now lies in about eight fathoms of water [48 feet]." (Courtesy of Kim Brungraber.)

This sailor's hat was found on the *May Queen*. The report continued, "The little vessel was in tow of the tug *J. Doyan* at the time, when all at once the former sprung a leak and went down so suddenly that those on board were unable to clear the yawl boat from the davits, and they found themselves floundering in the water. As soon as the condition of things was discovered, the tug immediately put out a boat and the imperiled seamen were rescued in nearly an exhausted condition." (Courtesy of Kim Brungraber.)

A lantern, bowls, plates, and cups are some of the artifacts in the stern area of the sunken vessel. The *May Queen* and its cargo of salted fish was valued at $1,500, all uninsured. Lindquist may have been in pursuit of purchasing the *May Queen*, but it was never put on paper. A salvage attempt was made the following spring. The steamer *J. F. Dayan* made an effort to recover the little vessel *May Queen* by dragging for the sunken schooner, but the search proved futile. A few weeks later, a third try was attempted and proved successful by a fisherman, and as soon as possible, efforts to raise the sunken craft were to be made. The papers were not surrendered until June 30, 1888, at Milwaukee—almost five years later—so the owners must have wanted to salvage it for a long time before giving up. The cause of surrender was "wrecked on Lake Michigan." The area that it sank was very active fishing grounds. In 2002, Bob Ruleau, who fishes commercially out of Cedar River, Michigan, snagged his nets on the old schooner. He had an underwater video camera, and set it down to see what he had caught up on. He was hooked on an old schooner—the *May Queen*—which his father had found while fishing almost 40 years earlier. (Courtesy of Kim Brungraber.)

Frontier Certificate of Enrollment,

№. *104*

OF THE

Schooner

May Queen

13 03/ Tons.
13 03/

ISSUED AT THE

Port of *Milwaukee*

District of *Milwaukee*

May 7th, 18*79*

John Nagro
Collector of Customs.

DATE OF SURRENDER:
June 30. 1888

WHERE SURRENDERED:
Milwaukee

CAUSE OF SURRENDER:
Wrecked on Lake
Michigan.

Collector of Customs.

Here is a copy of the enrollment certificate surrendered at Milwaukee on June 30, 1888. Ken Mortinson, a diver, first located the wreck in the fall of 2004. He was afraid of unscrupulous divers taking the fragile artifacts sighted at the wreck and left a sign: "Please take pictures only." (Courtesy of National Archives.)

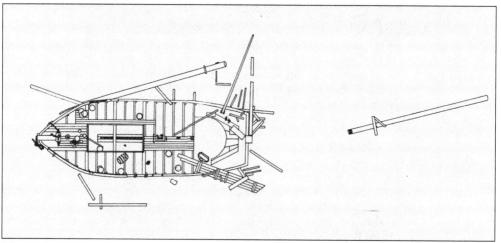

This preliminary site plan was drawn by Wayne Lusardi, maritime archeologist, with the state of Michigan Arts and Libraries. Lusardi had this to say of the new find: "Small, vernacular sailing craft are not well represented in the archaeological record, and the discovery of *May Queen* affords a unique opportunity to study a little known vessel type . . . many of its artifacts remain in place . . . and [its] importance to . . . regional maritime history cannot be overstated." (Courtesy of Wayne Lusardi.)

The *Erie L. Hackley*—the bay's biggest maritime disaster—is seen here in its original configuration. The *Erie L. Hackley* was built by J. Arnold in 1882 as a steam yacht at Muskegon, Michigan. The original dimensions were 79 feet in length, 17.33 feet in beam, a 5.16-foot depth of hold, and 54.61 gross tons. In 1899, it was converted to a small packet steamer by adding a deck and a raised pilothouse. The gross tonnage changed to 91 tons. It would shuttle freight and passengers in Lower Michigan. (Courtesy of TBRC.)

The *Erie L. Hackley* is pictured after the conversion to a packet steamer. It was purchased in May 1903 for $3,000 from parties in Charlevoix, Michigan, to become the first and only vessel in the newly formed Fish Creek Transportation Company. It would run up the west coast of the peninsula from Egg Harbor, Fish Creek, Ephraim, Sister Bay, Ellison Bay, and Detroit Harbor on Washington Island to Menominee and Sturgeon Bay. (Courtesy of DCMM.)

This old-fashioned funeral possession, including a horse-drawn hearse and period dress, took place on May 10, 1986, for the skeletal remains of two unidentified victims of the *Hackley* disaster. At 5:05 p.m. on October 3, 1903, the *Hackley* left Menominee for Egg Harbor. The wind was southwest and blowing hard. They were north of Green Island, about eight miles out, when they were hit by a fierce storm that laid the *Hackley* over in the trough of the sea, and from this it would never recover. The boat sank within two minutes, the pilothouse breaking off and 19 passengers and crew left to the cold waters. There were many stories of heroism and many of sadness told by the eight survivors (four passengers and four crew members). Edna and Ethel Vincent were sisters planning on visiting their mother in Fish Creek—the two were last seen clinging to each other before the seas washed them away. Lawrence Barringer was last seen trying to save his sister Edna—both drowned. Over half of the 11 fatalities were from Fish Creek. One owner of the *Hackley*, Edgar Thorp, was in Menominee and planned on returning to Fish Creek aboard the *Hackley*, but the foul-looking weather at the time made him change his mind. The steamer *Sheboygan* came across the wreckage at 8:00 the following morning and rescued the eight survivors from the floating cabin they had clung to for over 14 hours. (Courtesy of Gary K. Soule.)

Above, the casket is removed from the horse-drawn hearse. Below, the pine casket is being entombed at Bayside Cemetery in Sturgeon Bay. During the salvage, many artifacts were brought up, and the skeletal remains of two victims were found. These were brought to Sturgeon Bay and for six years left at a mortuary until 1986. The mortuary donated a casket, plot, and marker for the two victims. In Wisconsin, there are laws now that protect shipwrecks that have a loss of life as a burial site, and they cannot be disturbed. (Courtesy of Gary K. Soule.)

The schooner *Iver Lawson* is seen on the southern shore of Horseshoe Bay. A huge storm of October 19, 1905, did considerable damage on all the Great Lakes. There were 21 lives lost, and 30 vessels were lost or severely damaged, totaling over $500,000 in shipping losses. Capt. Henry Larson of Chicago owned the *Iver Lawson*. It left the port on the morning of October 17, bound for Masonville, Michigan, and was forced to seek shelter from a storm shortly after leaving Bear Lake. After the storm, it proceeded on the trip, and by the night of October 19, it had cleared Death's Door with the wind out of the northeast. The wind suddenly shifted to the north and blew a gale of hurricane strength. The *Iver Lawson* lost all of its canvas, leaving it to the mercy of the wind and waves. They drifted for several hours before the vessel was thrown high onto the southern shore of Horseshoe Bay. The crew could not see in the storm and stayed onboard overnight; in the morning, they were amazed at their predicament and relieved to be safe. Captain Larson and his crew of three were taken to Sturgeon Bay. They had only the clothes on their backs, and the vessel that was valued at $1,800 had no insurance. Their immediate needs were taken care of, and passage back to Chicago was arranged for on one of the Goodrich steamers the following day. (Courtesy of DCMM.)

Here is the stern view of the *Iver Lawson* at Horseshoe Bay. Nothing was done to release the vessel immediately, and with an offshore wind, a person could walk all the way around the vessel without getting their feet wet—at the time a peculiar spectacle. It was, however, not badly damaged in the incident, and several parties were interested in buying it. In May 1906, Capt. David Ramage of Sturgeon Bay purchased it from Captain Larson, with the intention of refloating it, but attempts by the tug *Torrent* to pull the vessel off the shore failed; Captain Ramage was nevertheless stuck with the $200 towing bill. (Courtesy of DCMM.)

Here is the bow view of the *Iver Lawson* at Horseshoe Bay. In July 1908, work again commenced on pulling the *Lawson*, now owned by Norman Mathieson from Bayfield, Wisconsin, to deep water. The steamer *Reliable* was pulling on the vessel when the *Lawson* fell off its ways, and again work was stopped. No other attempts were made, and it was dismantled on the beach. The Miller brothers built the *Iver Lawson* at Chicago in 1869. It was 117.66 feet long, had a 25.58-foot beam, with a 9.42 depth of hold, and 170.15 gross tons. It originally had two masts but was rigged to a three-masted vessel in 1888. (Courtesy of DCMM.)

Four

THE JOURNEY ENDS
STURGEON BAY

The *Joseph L. Hurd* had a very troubled career on the Great Lakes. Besides the accidents mentioned in this book, it had many difficulties, some that involved death to some of its crew. Capt. Edward Carus put it best: "The *Hurd*'s sister ship the *Phil Sheridan*, had equally as black a record on the lower lakes."

The bark *Two Friends* was given up for total loss in North Bay after the Alpena Blow of 1880 (and many books still place it there). But in 1881, it was recovered and was placed in dry dock at Milwaukee. The vessel required an entire new bottom, new keel, new keelson, new deadwood aft, new jib boom, spars, rudder, rudderposts, and new outfit of canvas. The bark *Two Friends* was rechristened the schooner *Pewaukee*. Door County had another bad storm on October 26, 1887, and the *Pewaukee* went on Detroit Island reef near Washington Island and once again was abandoned to the underwriters. Leathem and Smith ended up purchasing the craft from the underwriters and made the vessel into a steam-powered schooner. The work was completed in 1888, and it was the first schooner to have steam power added on, in the upper lakes. This was deemed a success but would not last long, and the ship's rig was changed to a steam barge in the winter of 1889.

The wreck of the *Vermillion* was for a long time thought to be that of the steam barge *Mueller*. (It also is listed to be out at the quarry in many books.) But the truth is the *Mueller* was dismantled and salvaged at Bay Shipbuilding Inc. Its stern was donated to the Door County Maritime Museum and is now located at the quarry where the vessel's remains were once believed to be.

The schooner *Lucia A. Simpson* sat at the shipyard until 1932 when the Town Harbor Yacht Club had plans to bring it to Chicago for a floating headquarters. It was found to be in bad shape below the waterline. This plan went to waste because the group could not afford to see its completion. By 1934, the *Simpson* was the last commercial sailing vessel on the lakes and being built in Manitowoc, Wisconsin, and the local Lions Club sponsored a movement to bring the ship home and make it a maritime museum. Fire would consume the last of the white-winged warriors in 1935.

As it appeared in 1933, the remains of the *Vermillion* can be seen on the beach to the right. Thomas Smith and John Leathem started the Leathem and Smith Quarry in 1893. By 1901, John Leathem left the firm, which included a very successful towing and wrecking company, and Smith had engaged in almost every resource the county had ever exploited including ice, lumber, shipbuilding, and now stone. His was the biggest quarry to date operating in Sturgeon Bay. At least seven ships lay somewhere at the quarry, but only two are evident in the water today. In 1903, Smith would bring three abandoned schooners—the *Bay State*, the *Emerald*, and the *Kate Hinchman*—out to the quarry to build a dock that extended to the deeper water. Thomas Smith would die in 1914, and his son Leathem D. Smith (named after his longtime partner, John Leathem) would take over all operations. Leathem would sell the quarry in 1927, and the new company from Ohio would name the quarry the Sturgeon Bay Company and would operate until 1944 when they moved the equipment to Drummond Island. (Courtesy of DCMM.)

The *Joseph L. Hurd* is seen here as it looked in its original form in the Chicago River. The *Joseph L. Hurd* was built in 1869 by Gordon Cambell in Detroit. It was 171 feet long, with a 29.2-foot beam, and a depth of 10.9 feet at 759.88 gross tons. It was built as a packet freighter to haul freight and passengers in the Great Lakes. On November 8, 1877, a fierce storm arose on Lake Michigan. The Canadian schooner *Magellan*, bound from Chicago to Toronto with a load of corn, washed ashore between Two Rivers and Manitowoc, Wisconsin. Badly broken up and with the loss of all eight hands aboard, speculation was that it had a collision out on the lake and sank very quickly. The *Hurd* came into Manitowoc a short time later with the bow badly damaged. Later in November, the *Inter Ocean* reported that the owners and the insurance company of the *Magellan* were to have a diver examine it. Although there were plenty of accusations against the *Hurd* for sinking the schooner, no official investigation was ever conducted and no charges were ever brought against the captain or crew. (Courtesy of TBRC.)

This is an artist's conception of the *Cayuga*. On May 10, 1895, the *Hurd* would run into the new steel steamer *Cayuga*. In a dense fog near Charlevoix, Michigan, the two vessels mistook passing signals, and the wooden *Hurd* rammed the *Cayuga* by the starboard bow, penetrating the steel hull and tearing the bow off the *Hurd* just forward of its bulkhead. The *Cayuga* sank quickly, and the crew in the lifeboats came aboard the *Hurd*. (Courtesy of TBRC.)

The *Hurd* is seen here being towed into Harbor Springs by the tug *Favorite*. (Courtesy of TBRC.)

The *Hurd* is seen with its bow broken off from the collision with the *Cayuga*. The captain of the *Hurd*, after the accident, ran full speed for the nearest harbor. Finally, the captain drove the craft onto the nearest beach in fear of sinking in deeper water. The cook on the *Hurd* jumped into the water and drowned—the only casualty of the sinking. The *Hurd* would stay on the beach until August 1895, when it was sold under the marshal's hammer for $750 to Leathem and Smith Towing and Wrecking Company. It was raised and brought to Manitowoc for repairs. Thomas Smith had new ideas for his steamer and removed the center arch bracing and eliminated the upper deck to resemble a steam barge. Meanwhile, the Reed Wrecking Company was attempting to raise the *Cayuga* and had many problems, including the loss of divers working on the wreck. It was never raised. Between the vessel and cargo, it was a $250,000 loss, compared to the *Hurd*, which was valued at $15,000. (Courtesy of TBRC.)

The *Hurd* is pictured here loaded with lumber. It could carry 725,000 feet in one trip and was loaded 19 feet over the top rail. It was the most costly ship of the fleet as far as fuel went, and there were many alterations to the vessel to solve this. In 1897, they placed one of the salvaged boilers from the *Australasia* on the *Hurd* to give it more power. The *Hurd* also carried stone that year but stayed primarily in the lumber business until 1906—another cursed year for the ship. In April 1906, its captain had a fatal accident. In June, a deckhand fell to his death. In August, it ran aground at Racine. (Courtesy of DCMM.)

The *Hurd* is pictured here loading stone at the Leathem and Smith Quarry. This is the dock it was tied up at when it was lost. The final blow came on September 22, 1913, when a gale blowing out of the northwest parted the mooring lines and was blown up on the beach. The *Hurd* was partially loaded with stone and pounding on the bottom. The pumps ran, but to no avail, and the old ship broke its back from the strain. The enrollment papers were surrendered in Milwaukee on November 10, 1913, stating "stranded (total loss)." (Courtesy of TBRC.)

At its final resting place, Leathem and Smith Quarry, behind the *Pewaukee*, is seen the self-unloading schooner *Adriatic* being loaded with crushed stone, around 1914. The schooner *Two Friends*—built in 1875, sunk and abandoned in 1880 but recovered in 1881—was rechristened the *Pewaukee* and was valued at $15,000. It was rebuilt in Milwaukee by Wolf and Davidson and served well for several years. But Door County had another bad storm on October 26, 1887, and the *Pewaukee* went on Detroit Island reef near Washington Island. This time, its owners abandoned the craft to the underwriters and surrendered the enrollment papers at the port of Milwaukee on November 4, 1887. Leathem and Smith ended up purchasing the craft from the underwriters for $6,000 and making it into a steam-powered schooner. Under the right conditions, the *Pewaukee* could sail, and if the wind was not cooperating, it would switch to steam. The work was completed in 1888, and it became the first schooner to have steam power added on to sail the upper lakes. This was deemed a success but would not last long, as its rig was changed to a steam barge in the winter of 1889. (Courtesy of DCMM.)

Pictured here is the bow of the *Pewaukee* near the crushed stone loading conveyer at the Leathem and Smith Quarry. In the winter of 1898, the *Pewaukee* was converted into an unrigged tow barge. It would work as a tow barge until 1905, when the machinery was removed and it was converted into a barge for the stone trade. It worked in the stone trade hauling stone to Manitowoc, Ludington, Grand Haven, and various ports around Lake Michigan until being relegated to the boneyard in 1912. Here the *Pewaukee* would be shoved up into the mud at the foot of Liberty Street. By this time, the Leathem and Smith Quarry was producing crushed rock, and the waste from this would get washed into the bay in high winds and storms. This caused a problem in that it would force much dredging to facilitate ships to get close enough to the pier to be loaded. The *Pewaukee* would be called into service one last and final time. So, the *Pewaukee* ended its long career 33 years after it was condemned the first time, 26 years after its enrollments were surrendered in Milwaukee, and 40 years after it was originally built in Canada as the *Two Friends*. On November 10, 1913, the enrollments were surrendered at Milwaukee the same day as the *Hurd's*. (Courtesy of DCMM.)

In this photograph, taken sometime between 1904 and 1912, the *Vermillion* has only two of its original four masts. It was built as the *J. C. Gilchrist* at Trenton, Michigan, by John Craig and Sons, master builders, in 1887. It was 252 feet in length with a 42-foot beam and 20.4-foot depth. It was 1,827.39 gross tons and 1,395.75 net tons. It was listed as a propeller with two decks, four masts, a plain head, and a round stern. On March 25, 1904, the *J. C. Gilchrist* became the *Vermillion* in Cleveland, Ohio. The Gilchrist Transportation Company by this time was trying to get a monopoly on Great Lakes shipping. This did not happen, and in the process, the company overexpanded, went into bankruptcy, and auctioned off much of its fleet. The *Vermillion* was purchased for a very low price by the Milwaukee Iron Works, which salvaged the engine and boilers. The papers were surrendered in Cleveland, Ohio, on March 18, 1913. The final blow to the *Vermillion* came in 1915: "Vessel out of commission and on February 23, 1915 reportedly abandoned." The old hull lay sunk in the Milwaukee River until the spring of 1917 when the harbor commission decided to get rid of it. Leathem D. Smith saw the *Vermillion* as an inexpensive way to add to his stone fleet and purchased the hull from the city for a token amount. (Courtesy of DCMM.)

The barge *Interlaken* is loading crushed stone at the Leathem and Smith Quarry with the hull of the *Vermillion* pictured in the foreground. The tug *Hunsader* towed the loaded stone carriers *Dohearty* and *City of Glasgow* to Milwaukee the last week of May 1917 and returned with the hull of the *Vermillion*. Back at the yard of the Leathem and Smith Company, the craft was sunk to a predetermined depth and the upper works burned off as part of a Fourth of July celebration, and after that, it was allowed to sink to the bottom once again. In 1920, the hull was raised once more for the intention of making it into a graving dock. But by November, it had sunk again, and now Leathem Smith did not plan to raise it unless he planned on pushing shipbuilding and would use it as a floating dry dock. However, in February 1923, Smith patented his first self-unloading system and because of its success, needed all available slips—the steamer *Vermillion* was to be raised, one last time, for a breakwater. (Courtesy of DCMM.)

Here is the stern of the wreck at the south end of the quarry. Note the plug half buried for propeller shaft. That was installed in Milwaukee where its machinery was salvaged.

Built in 1868 by R. Hayes of Fairport, Ohio, the scow schooner *Dan Hayes* was first owned by Hayes and Fountain, also of Fairport. The vessel was 112 feet in length, 24.16 feet in beam, with a 7-foot depth of hold. Originally three-masted, the *Dan Hayes* had a gross tonnage of 145.96 tons. During its early career, the vessel operated chiefly in the lumber trade and often visited the port of Milwaukee. On August 3, 1898, while en route from Manistee to Milwaukee with a load of bark, the *Hayes* was caught in an unexpected summer storm and suffered the worst damage of its sailing career. The vessel eventually sprung a leak just north of Milwaukee and became "waterlogged" (partially submerged but still afloat). According to the *Detroit Free Press*, Capt. Ole Oleson and the vessel's three crewmen abandoned the leaking vessel and spent five hours battling the sea in a small yawl before coming ashore. The *Hayes*, finally towed into Milwaukee by the tug *Simpson*, lost all three masts and its entire deck load of bark. Sustaining about $1,000 in damages, the *Hayes*'s active sailing career effectively came to an end as a result of the accident. (Courtesy of DCMM.)

In 1900, the Sturgeon Bay's Graef and Nebel stone quarry purchased the aging *Dan Hayes* in Milwaukee, paying only $226 for the dismasted schooner. After a thorough overhauling, including a new bow and planking, the vessel was put into the stone trade as a barge. Demonstrating the hazards of using older vessels as barges, the *Hayes* seems to have spent in inordinate amount of time being recaulked to prevent small leaks from sinking the vessel out of sight. On August 3, 1904, the tug *Duncan City* was to pick up the *Hayes* loaded with stone for Menominee but on arrival found that the scow was leaking so badly that it had to be shoved up on shore to prevent it from sinking completely. The Sturgeon Bay Stone Company would not allocate any more funds for the *Hayes* to be raised and repaired. Six years to the date of the *Dan Hayes* losing its sailing career, its second life as a barge would end. By 1905, the *Dan Hayes* was resting on the bottom of Sturgeon Bay. (Courtesy of Patrick Labadie.)

The steam barge *S. C. Baldwin*, schooner *Ida Corning*, and tug *Torrent* are pictured here tied up at the Sturgeon Bay Stone Company dock. Bullhead Point started as a quarry operation by the name of Termansen and Jensen Company in 1898, until its merger with Graef and Nebel Company in January 1903. The new company went by the name of Sturgeon Bay Stone Company until the early 1930s when it stopped operations. Three ships were abandoned there—the *Empire State*, the *Ida Corning*, and the *Oak Leaf*. The *Empire State* caught fire in late July 1929, and in October 1931, the *Ida Corning* and the *Oak Leaf* were intentionally burned down to the waterline to prevent children from getting injured on the rotting decks of the old vessels. (Courtesy of DCMM.)

The *Oak Leaf* was built by Peck and Masters at Cleveland, Ohio, in 1866 as a three-masted schooner. It was 129.75 feet in length, 31 feet in beam with an 11.16-foot depth of hold, and a gross tonnage of 319.36 tons with a net of 303.4 tons. The schooner was built for Capt. Henry Kelly, who operated a small fleet that routinely traded between Lake Erie and Lake Michigan. Its first crew of six to eight men was under the command of Capt. Hugh Morrison, a one-armed man who knew the perils of the Great Lakes. (Courtesy of TBRC.)

The *Oak Leaf* (left) and the *I. N. Foster* are seen here unloading stone in Michigan. The *Oak Leaf* was rebuilt in July 1891 in Chicago. Its new dimensions were 160 feet in length, 31.16 feet in breadth, with a 10.58-foot depth of hold at 395.03 gross tons, and 375.28 net. The vessel was then considered a barge and had the main mast removed for easier loading and discharge of cargo. As a barge, the *Oak Leaf* would boost a crew of only three people, responsible mainly for checking and repairing leaks. The Sturgeon Bay Stone Company was awarded a large contract in Michigan, and because of this, they purchased the *Oak Leaf*. It had very little trouble other than an occasional storm or minor collision and would haul stone until 1920. It was retired at the quarry pier in the mid- to late 1920s until the fire in 1931. (Courtesy of DCMM.)

The schooner *Ida Corning* is pictured in the lumber trade. It was built by Thomas Arnold and M. J. Rodgers at East Saginaw, Michigan, in 1881. It was 168 feet in length, 31.3-foot beam with a 10.9-foot depth of hold, and a gross tonnage of 444 tons with a net of 422 tons. The *Corning* was built as a schooner barge and had a fore and a mizzenmast, which was typically called a Grand Haven Rig. The lack of a main mast (center mast) accommodated easier loading and kept the main deck open for cargo. It was designed to be towed and would only use its canvas in emergency or to assist in a tow. This was very practical for the lumber trade when the deck loads could be up to 30 to 40 percent of its total cargo. It was originally built for L. P. Mason and Company of East Saginaw and was constructed with an aft cabin and high forecastle deck forward to accommodate an anchor winch, and perhaps a small boiler and donkey engine. The *Ida Corning* would primarily be a lumber hooker for the first 27 years of its career, until purchased by the Sturgeon Bay Stone Company in March 1908. It would be towed by the tug *Duncan City* and the steam barge *I. N. Foster* in its early years for the quarry hauling stone to Holland and Ludington, Michigan. (Courtesy of TBRC.)

The steamer *Empire State* is seen in its original configuration. The *Empire State* was launched on April 5, 1862, for the Buffalo firm of Mason and Bidwell. It was 212 feet in length, 32.7 feet in beam with a 12.2-foot depth of hold, a gross tonnage of 1,116.53, and 962.8 net tons. It was built as a passenger freight steamer and was one of the finest vessels on the Great Lakes at the time. As a passenger freight steamer, it would transport freight below decks and passengers above and is reported to have carried many immigrants from the eastern states to the expanding west after the Civil War. The end of the vessel's career as a steamer came on Christmas Day in 1906, when a fire broke out in the engine room at the Barry Dock in Chicago after 44 years of service on the lakes. After the fire, the *Empire State* was purchased by the Schnorbeck and Bennet Company of Muskegon, Michigan, and converted into an unpowered tow barge to carry stone at Sturgeon Bay. It would haul stone from the Sturgeon Bay Stone Company to Holland, Michigan. In 1910, the Sturgeon Bay Stone Company purchased the *Empire State* for $2,500 along with the *Richard Mott*. The Sturgeon Bay Stone Company used the *Empire State* until the fire in 1929 after 67 years on the lakes; the *Ida Corning* and the *Oak Leaf* were also consumed by fire in 1931. (Courtesy of TBRC.)

Pictured here is the steamer *Joys*. It was built in Milwaukee in 1884 by Milwaukee Shipyard Company and was 131 feet in length and 28.16 feet in breadth with a 9.75-foot draft. It had a wood hull of 268.07 gross tons and 221.55 net. The steamer was built for Jas. Sheriff, who patented and manufactured the Sheriff Wheel's (propellers). By July 1897, it was engaged in the stone industry hauling about 70 cords of stone from Sturgeon Bay to Muskegon, Michigan. The contract for Muskegon government piers called for 1,500 cords, which would take the *Joys* about 22 round-trips to complete. By April 1898, the *Joys* was loading stone at the Termansen and Jensen Quarry (Bull Head Point) for a new government contract at Grand Haven, Michigan. It was also engaged in the lumber industry that year, but the good times for the *Joys* would be short-lived. (Courtesy of TBRC.)

The bow of the *Joys* is seen after the fire. On December 20, 1898, the *Joys*, put into the ship canal for weather on Thursday morning while on voyage to Menominee from Milwaukee for cargo, caught fire and was totally destroyed at its moorings at the westerly end of the cut at an early hour the following morning. (Courtesy of DCMM.)

Pictured is the burned and sunk hull of the *Joys*. The fire originated from the smokestack in the vicinity of the breaching, consuming the after cabin first. The fire was discovered by Captain Connelly, who saw the illumination from his room, and by the time he threw on his clothes and gave the alarm, the entire after end of the boat was a roaring mass of flames. The crew narrowly escaped from the burning craft with their lives, and the mate and steward, whose rooms were nearest to the fire, did not even have time to grab their clothes but jumped from the cabin to the ice in their bare feet with nothing on but their shirts. The flames spread so rapidly that by the time the crew got together, nothing whatsoever could be done toward subduing the element. The steward lost $40 in money, a gold watch, and about $75 worth of clothing. The mate lost all of his clothing and a gold watch. The firemen lost their clothing with the exception of the clothes they had on, having turned in standing. The captain saved the ship's papers but, with all the excitement, lost the books and most of the accounts. (Courtesy of DCMM.)

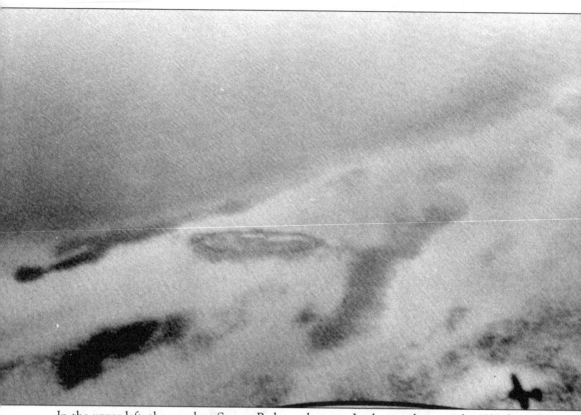

In the upper left, the wreck at Sunset Park can be seen. In the wreck report for 1898 from the *Door County Advocate*, Lake Michigan wrecks published the first week of January 1899, the *Joys* was listed as a $15,000 loss. The following week, a local vessel owner was reportedly looking at purchasing the hull to convert it to a stone barge, but it was also reported that the hull was in very poor shape. This was undoubtedly the Thomas Smith from the Leathem and Smith Towing and Wrecking Company that also owned a stone quarry, who would eventually get the job of salvaging it. The hull was stripped of all its machinery and any other things that could be salvaged and shoved onto Dunlap Reef. At this time, Leathem and Smith Company was talking about converting the partially burned steamer *Fountain City* into a floating dry dock. This was the same steamer that was always thought to be in front of Sunset Park. Also at this time, the company sealed the fate of the steamer *Joys*. According to the *Advocate* files, May 13, 1899, "The wreck of the steamer *Joys* has been utilized as a breakwater by the Pankratz Lumber Co. for the protection of their boomage located on the north side of their dock. The company is also thinking of pulling the wreck of the steamer Ira Chaffee off Dunlap reef for the same purpose."

The *Fountain City* was one of the earliest passenger and freight steamers on Lake Huron and Lake Michigan, seen here sometime between 1857 and 1895. It was built by pioneer shipbuilder Capt. E. M. Peck and Masters at Cleveland, Ohio, in 1857 at a cost of $40,000. It originally measured 209.92 feet in length, with a 30.25-foot beam, and a 13.5-foot depth of 820.40 gross tons. Peck and Masters also built the *R. J. Hackett* and *Empire State*, both sunk in Door County waters. (Courtesy of DCMM.)

The *Fountain City* is seen after a fire in May 1896. It was rebuilt in early 1895 and had its staterooms removed to accommodate more cargo. It was purchased in April 1895 by Benjamin F. Davison of Chicago, to be used in the lumber trade in Menominee. Capt. Charles A. Graves would be master. In early July 1895, a lamp exploded and did considerable damage when on its way to Chicago with a load of lumber. In March 1896, it was to have its large wooden arches removed and taken to Manitowoc for a overhauling. At this time, the *Fountain City* was valued at $6,000 and Capt. M. Clark was to be its master that season. By May, the work finally started on taking the arches out but was stopped, and it was returned to its winter mooring position. About 11:00 on the night of May 5, 1896, a fire alarm was sounded, and shortly after, the entire stern of the vessel was ablaze. (Courtesy of TBRC.)

The *Fountain City* is seen after it had been abandoned in the boneyard. The fire department arrived on the scene but was unable to reach the vessel, so they put the hose on a yawl boat and paid it out to the burning craft. They succeeded in putting out the fire, but the entire stern of the craft was destroyed. The owners stated that an anchor light that was maintained on the vessel exploded and started the fire. It had a four-month insurance policy on it for $4,000, which would have ran out the next week. The enrollment papers were surrendered May 16 in Milwaukee, and the insurance was adjusted to $3,500. Some of its machinery was removed in 1898 to be used on the steam barge *Hurd*. By 1899, there was talk of raising it and making a floating dry dock from the hull for servicing tugs. Also in 1899, vessel men were complaining that the *Fountain City* was an obstruction to navigation, along with the schooner *Pride* that sank nearby. Captain Isabell, in 1901, placed bulkheads in the stern of it so it could be raised, but this was never accomplished, and it would eventually be filled over and probably lies under the present-day Bay Shipbuilding property. (Courtesy of TBRC.)

The *Lucia A. Simpson* is seen with all its canvas and a full deck load of cargo. The ship was built by Rand and Burger at its yard in Manitowoc in 1875. It measured 127 feet in length, 28 feet in beam, with 8.58-foot depth of hold at 227 gross tons. Most of its life was spent in the lumber trade, hauling timber products from northern ports to Chicago and Milwaukee. The *Simpson* had little trouble in its life and was a profitable craft for the vessel's owners. (Courtesy of TBRC.)

The *Simpson* is seen at port in the late 1920s. It was only one of four commercial working sail craft on the Great Lakes and was sold to a group of men who had a bold plan for the schooner that was not profitable as a commercial carrier. The group fitted out the vessel with diving equipment, hoisting equipment and other salvage tools. The plan was to seek out sunken wrecks in Lake Huron and Lake Superior for their valuable cargos. (Courtesy of TBRC.)

The *Lucia A. Simpson* sits at the shipyard in Sturgeon Bay. The *Simpson* set sail from Milwaukee in July 1929, headed for St. Ignace, Michigan. It was making good time and running in full canvas when hit by a sudden squall that broke the vessel's mizzenmast off and opened its seams. The crew quickly cut the rigging away and manned the pumps while sounding the distress signal. The *Ann Arbor* heard the call and came to assist and immediately wired the Kewaunee Coast Guard, who came out and took the vessel to the Kewaunee harbor. Later the tug *Sunbeam* would tow the *Simpson* to Sturgeon Bay where it was put into the boxes for a check of its haul. In December 1935, a fire broke out at the Sturgeon Bay Shipbuilding and Dry Dock Company. In all, seven vessels were destroyed or badly damaged, among them the *Simpson*. This would be the end to one of the last of the windjammers of the Great Lakes. (Courtesy of DCMM.)

Visit us at
arcadiapublishing.com

CPSIA information can be obtained
at www.ICGtesting.com
Printed in the USA
LVHW061459180723
752687LV00009B/758